MARY BROWN'S HANDBOOK

BERNICE BLOOM

Bernice Bloom

SECTION ONE

THIS IS MY OFFICIAL HANDBOOK

This is my Official Handbook

A reference book packed with basic rules for coping as a fat girl in a thin world.

A book which puts larger ladies' needs, hopes and dreams first. It advises smiles, confidence and laughter in the face of an increasingly hostile society.

It's packed with tips and advice and a few angry rants at the world. Above all, I hope this book will make you feel better and smile a little.

Join me and lots of other readers on:

Facebook:
https://www.facebook.com/BerniceBloombooks

Twitter:
https://twitter.com/Bernice1Bloom

Instagram:
https://www.instagram.com/bernicebloomwriter

www.bernicebloom.com

INTRODUCTION

INTRODUCTION

It's just after 6 p.m. on a warm summer's evening, and I'm sitting on a bench enjoying the last of the sun's rays while waiting for a friend. As I'm sitting here, two women walk down the street towards me, talking animatedly and laughing at some private joke. They look as if they are enjoying life, laughing and clinging to one another as they recall some funny moment or humorous comment from their past. They are dressed well, one in a long kaftan-style dress, and the other in three-quarter length white trousers and a gorgeous emerald green flowing top. They wear simple white plimsolls that allow them to dance along in the early evening warmth. They look happy, and I find myself smiling as I watch their playful interactions, and think of my own friends, and how much fun we have.

The women spot a hot dog stand nearby, and join the small queue waiting for food. Before long they are both holding big hot dogs teeming with onions, ketchup and mustard. They sit down at the metal table and chairs next to the hot dog kiosk and enjoy their food with a bottle of beer each. They look so happy, so comfortable in their friendship and delighting in the world. The sight of them makes me feel uplifted.

The same cannot be said for the lady sitting next to me on the bench.

"I don't know what they've got to be so happy about," she says.

Her attention has been drawn by these women too. "I'm not sure I'd be smiling so much if I was that fat. And I certainly wouldn't be eating a huge hot dog like that. It's disgusting. People should get a grip on themselves."

I stare at the lady whose words have broken the magic of the moment, then look back over at the women. They're still laughing and joking with one another, and finishing off their snacks. They don't know they are being talked about in this cruel manner by the lady next to me, but in many ways – deep down – they *do* know. They know that every time they leave the house, someone, somewhere will disapprove of them.

If you are overweight, you will know what I mean. Everyone who is obese has become accustomed to the glances, the whispered comments and hidden criticism.

I wrote in one of my novels that "every overweight woman has cried in a changing room" and I didn't necessarily even mean it literally. I meant that there are shared experiences of hurt among those who are overweight, that thinner people will never know about.

We live in a world in which youth, wealth and thinness are treated as if they are as important as kindness, generosity and friends. To be overweight is to be considered 'less than' someone who is thin. It's the greatest irony that a 200 lb woman is twice the size of a 100 lb woman, but the 200 lb woman will be considered 'less than' in the western world.

Why is this?

Is it because in a world full of plenty, a figure which indicates that you don't indulge is more impressive than one which suggests that you do? Just as in a world with nothing, a figure which indicates that you do indulge is considered attractive and far superior.

I'm not being naive. I know there are other issues at play here, and of course being overweight can be one of the factors when it comes to serious health issues. There is undoubtedly a link between obesity and ill health. But it would be remarkably unfair to conclude therefore that all overweight people are unhealthy and those who aren't overweight are without medical issues. There's a relationship between obesity and health but it's not intrinsic and it's not always a straightforward causal one.

In any case, the opprobrium heaped on overweight people is out of proportion to any damage they are doing, and all of that potential damage is to themselves and not to those around them.

The lovely ladies sitting by the roadside eating their hot dogs are not causing me any discomfort. Further along the bench a man is smoking. Clearly the smoke he is inhaling will damage him, but the smoke he exhales will damage me as well. Accident and emergency departments are filled with people who have been hurt by drunks; drunk drivers fight, argue and kill people on the roads.

Society heaps opprobrium on these people too, but

that's because they are hurting people. What are overweight people doing that's so awful? You can argue that they cost the NHS a lot of money every year, and they do; there's no question about that. But so do smoking, drugs and alcohol. I genuinely think we have a reaction to overweight people that is out of kilter, so let's take a deeper look at the whole thing.

Appearances are everything

The reason overweight people are commented on and treated with disdain is because you can see weight gain so clearly, leading to the assumption that those carrying extra pounds overeat. This is not always the situation, of course: medicines and illness can lead to weight gain. But those who do overeat find that every extra calorie they consume shows up and marks them out as physically different from those who do not overeat. They stand out. I think the vilification of the overweight is as much about them being seen as unsightly, and physically repugnant to some people, as it is about them being seen as unable to control themselves.

The impact of gambling, smoking, drinking and drug taking is not necessarily visible until the person is a long way down the road towards addiction. The same cannot be said of eating. The signs are there straight away and are visible every day. A drunk will sober up, a drug addict will come down off his high, but overeating leaves an instant mark… It's easier to see their 'problem' and easier to mock it. I am not suggesting for a second that drinking and drug taking are consequence-free, not at all, but it's the cumulative effect that causes damage, over years, and the damage can be hidden until the illness is advanced. Those who overeat are thrown into a cycle of guilt and shame much faster and more publicly.

Food is everywhere

It's no surprise that obesity numbers are growing at a time when food, cooking and baking are more popular than ever.

There have never been so many food choices available, and the most popular shows on television are programmes like *Great British Bake Off*, *Nigella Kitchen* and *MasterChef*. Or there's *Come Dine with Me*, *Dinner Date* and *Ready Steady Cook*. And just try finding anything but cooking shows on television on a Sunday morning. It's wall-to-wall *Sunday Brunch* and *John & Lisa's Weekend Kitchen*.

Cooking and food are all around us like it never has been in the past. The majority of people alive in the West today are from the first generation of people for whom food has always been plentiful. No rationing, no shortages, no wars or strikes that have stopped food production. Food is everywhere like never before in the history of mankind.

But, our desire to be thin has never been greater.

Conspiracy theory

It's like this bizarre conspiracy. Hey, let's fill the streets with truly delicious food, make takeaways available at the touch of a phone and flaunt food across every television station all the time, and then expect people to be slim, and tutt at them aggressively if they're not. I wonder how smokers would cope under the same pressure – if there were television programmes on constantly about how lovely it was to smoke, full of tips to make smoking as delicious as possible, and the ability to order cigarettes to your front door in 20 minutes at any time.

Added to all this is the important fact that losing weight is much more complicated than giving up smoking or drinking because you can't just stop doing it like you do with smoking.

Imagine if you had to drink alcohol to survive, but only certain types of it and only in certain quantities or you'd be squawked at in public and ridiculed endlessly?

That's how it feels for the overweight.

And while the number of fast-food outlets explodes through the ceiling, the programmes on the TV multiply and shops offer three-for-the-price-of-one deals, all we want is to be slim and healthy.

And we want that quite badly. When surveys are conducted in which they ask people what they would most like to happen to them, the reply is not a desire for love, children, better health for elderly relatives or peace on earth. 'I want to lose a stone' always comes out top. When *Cosmopolitan* magazine put Tess Holliday, the plus-size model, on their front cover, there was absolute outrage. How could we possibly look up to someone who is overweight? Thin is the goal; thinness is to be celebrated.

The handbook

This little handbook aims to look at the whole world of being overweight: the awkward situations, the odd reactions and what you can do about them. It's a mixture of light-hearted observations and silliness to cheer you up, and more serious sections to rally you, and hopefully make you feel better about the world. There's also a workbook at the end which asks you to write down your thoughts and observations on the subjects you've read about.

I hope it will leave you nodding in recognition at the people, places and scenarios it features and smiling warmly at the assessments and warnings. But also moved to challenge outdated stereotypes.

It's a book for overweight women who want to scream: "I'm sorry my weight offends you so much. Your f***ing attitude offends me." It's for women who reach for the biscuits after a stressful phone call and can only mark the transition between work and home once they have a glass of wine in hand, and something delicious to eat on the table in front of them. It doesn't advocate obesity. But nor does it advocate hating yourself because you are obese. It's also about learning that no matter how hard you try; you will never hate your body into good health. No amount of scolding, shame, or abuse will make you thin.

If you want to feel better and start eating better, your body needs love and understanding. Despite what the woman on the bench may have thought on that warm evening as she watched those two women enjoying their hot dogs, eating too much doesn't make you a bad person. It just means you eat too much. That's all. It's not the biggest crime in the world, and overweight people should not be treated as criminals

I hope you enjoy the book.

BB xx

SECTION TWO

GENERAL OBSERVATIONS

POPULAR MYTHS

Myths about weight loss fly around the place like midges in the summertime, and they can be every bit as irritating. Their main role appears to be to make overweight people feel even worse about themselves than they do already. Where do these myths come from? No one really knows. Here are five of the main culprits.

1. I don't know what the problem is. Weight loss is straightforward: it's just 'calories in v calories out'

No it bloody well isn't. There's always one person in every group who'll say this, like we are overweight because we can't add up. No – this is not a maths problem – this is a cultural, social and emotional problem.

The statement will be uttered after someone makes a comment about how hard it is for them to lose weight, or has the audacity to talk about how they quit dieting altogether because it was stressing them out, and in comes *that* guy who says, "It's not hard if you really work for it – it's just making sure you burn more calories than you eat. Keep a note of how much you're eating and how much you're exercising."

That is *such* an insultingly drastic oversimplification – food affects all of our bodies in really different ways – and it's supposed to. We all come from different genetic backgrounds, and there are any number of hormone-related complications that can make losing weight difficult. Losing weight is hard.

Distance yourself from these people immediately, and build a wall around yourself if necessary. Whatever you do – don't talk to them.

2. You should dress for the body you have; not the body you want

Yeah, yeah, yeah. We all get this, but dressing as an overweight person is fraught with difficulty. So much so that there's a whole separate section on it in this book. It also features frequently in my series of novels, because it's such a tough thing to get right.

If you dress in big, baggy clothes, people will say you're not trying your best to look good, anything remotely tight will see you castigated for not dressing for your shape. I don't know what the rules are, you don't know what the rules are. Heavens, but there seem to be rules.

What are these rules?

Is baggy good or does it just make you look fatter? Is it true that vertical stripes are better than horizontal? Are dark colours better than light ones? If my body is apple-shaped I should wear one style, if I'm a triangle I should wear another? I have short legs so I shouldn't wear dresses past my knees, and my stomach is round so I should avoid anything attention grabbing. I definitely shouldn't wear swimsuits or sleeveless tops ever. Or should I?

I tell you what: I'm writing the handbook, so I'm writing the rules. The new rules are these: wear whatever the hell makes you comfortable and happy. There. That's it. Official.

3. Overweight women are more of a problem than overweight men

Now, I thought I'd include this because it is very interesting: research students at Seattle University investigated the differing attitudes to overweight men and overweight women. They came up with lots of conclusions that are sprinkled through the book, but one thing they established was that overweight men tend to be mocked by their peers; while overweight women are pitied.

Let's just let that sink in.

So, if you are an overweight man, people are more likely to call you 'tubby' or 'big man' and laugh about your size with you, whereas if you are female, people are more likely to feel sorry for you, and be very glad that they are not like you.

Now, I have no desire to be mocked for my size, but I don't much like the idea of being pitied either.

If you think about people caught up in major world events – they are the ones we feel pity towards. You would never mock people injured in the line of duty; you would feel enormous pity. Pity is the emotion saved for serious issues. You might mock someone who tripped over in front of you, but you'd feel desperately sorry for them if they broke their leg. When it's serious, the mocking stops and the pity starts.

Does this mean that women's weight is seen as being more serious than men's? Well, d'uh! Yes. There is no question. I think one of the great myths of being overweight is that it is seen much more as being a female issue than a male one.

But this is crazy. If you are going to argue that obesity is a bad thing, then you will say things like – it costs the National Health Service a fortune, it leads to illness, it stops you being active and playing with your kids, it reduces your life expectancy… All of these things apply to both sexes equally. The only reason people see overweight women as being 'worse' than overweight men is because we have such a huge obsession with women's looks. Another interesting thing to note here is that although men are more likely to mock and joke, when you look up 'fat jokes' most of them are about women! Mother-in-law and wife jokes abound.

Here are the two which occur most frequently:

Fat women shouldn't be mocked – don't you think they have enough on their plates?

Your mum's so fat...when she fell down the stairs, I thought East Enders was ending.

So, the conclusion is: men josh with each other and take the mickey, women are treated with pity, and comedians then focus on fat women when they make fat jokes.

4. 'FAT' is a synonym for 'ugly'

"Ugh, I'm so fat. Just look at me?"

I can't tell you the number of times I've heard something like that when women gather in ladies' rooms and changing rooms. Listen to yourself when you use the word 'fat'. Can you replace it with the words 'ugly', 'disgusting', 'lazy', etc? If so, that's exactly what you're calling all of your fat friends.

Fat is just a descriptive word – it doesn't mean everything bad in the world. It doesn't mean anything other than that you are carrying more weight in the form of fat cells. Try to use the word like that, rather than as a catch-all for ugly.

5. There is such a thing as the 'right' kind of fat person

There's a new person in town: the 'right' kind of fat person. Since people started thinking a little before using derogatory words about the overweight, and since plus-size models are making their presence felt, a slow, gentle acceptance has been growing for overweight people, but only the 'right kind'. Someone who is fat but goes to aerobics, dances, comes out to clubs and parties or is a plus-size model. These fat people are the right kind.

It's a disgrace. All people are equal. No one is more acceptable than anyone else.

There are lots of slim people who do very little and there are lots of overweight people who work hard and achieve a lot. Most of us are somewhere in the middle, making the best of life.

YOU KNOW YOU ARE FAT WHEN...

A handbook which aims to be a guide and companion for those who feel fat in a thin world is obliged to take a look at exactly what 'fat' means. How do you know when you're fat? I don't mean by looking at weight charts or measuring your BMI, I mean what happens socially and professionally to make you realise that people now see you as fat?

Let's take a look at some of the clues.

Being fat is:

- **The constant fear of breaking something because you're heavy**

WE'VE ALL BEEN THERE... That intake of breath you hear when you go to sit down on someone's new deckchair or lightweight dining chair. They smile, but their eyes are screaming, "For the love of God, don't sit on that. It's new and I love it and you're the size of a baby elephant and likely to rip it in two."

What the breath intakers don't realise is that every overweight person is also taking a silent breath when they sit on a flimsy chair and hoping with all their might that the thing doesn't collapse beneath them and send them crashing to the ground. However much the owner of the chair doesn't want the chair to be broken, the fat person wants it less.

My God, I've sat on flimsy chairs without putting any weight on them rather than risk them breaking. I've squatted like a weightlifter, or a holiday-maker using a French toilet, until my thighs have been shaking with pain, rather than risk one of the major fears of the larger lady: breaking something because of my weight.

- **Dreading shouts on the street**

YOU'RE WALKING along the street without a care in the world, watching as the birds swoop majestically through the cloudless sky when a cry drifts towards you: "Lose some weight lard-arse."

Marvellous: medical advice from passing van drivers. Just what we all need, a bit of drive-by counselling from a bloke who drinks 12 pints a night and chain-smokes his way through the day. You know he's only doing it to impress his mates, who probably aren't impressed at all, but laugh all the same.

You don't need me to tell you that you should ignore these absurd cries – they will only be injurious if you allow them to be. Just let them drift away from you – they are pointless and ridiculous. You won't ever be inspired to go to step aerobics and eat nothing but air-dried vegetables and grated ice cubes because a bloke in ripped jeans, sporting misspelled tattoos shouted at you.

- **Coping with 'funny' nicknames**

THE SILLY NICKNAMES. That's when you know. Ah, you're calling me Twinkle Toes and Twiglet because I'm fat. How nice. Go to hell.

- **Being told that every little misdemeanour is because of your weight**

IF YOU'RE overweight it seems that every conceivable problem you face is because of your weight. Have you noticed that? I've started not wanting to go to the doctors, dentists or opticians. Can't sleep at night? *Perhaps you need to lose weight.* Car won't start? *Ah, that'll be because you need to lose weight.* House is a mess? *Yes, but I'm sure it wouldn't be if you lost a few pounds.*

- **Dealing with chafing**

WE'LL DEAL with this delicate little subject later, but I'm afraid it's a sign. And – my God – how much does it hurt?

As if someone has ground smashed glass into your inner thighs before coating them with vinegar.

- **Coping with seat belts**

YES, you definitely know you're fat when you find yourself fearing any occasion when you may be asked to wear a seat belt, life jacket, or harness of any kind. It won't fit.

"Try this," someone will say.

"No," you will reply. "Take a look at your harness and then a quick look at my arse. How in God's name are you going to get that child-sized device over this lorry-sized body? Don't make me try. Find a bigger one."

- **People assuming you are super strong**

BEING ASKED to open people's bottles for them, or open doors and carry boxes. Being larger makes people think you're stronger. I'm sorry to report that I'm not. I just ate too many cakes; I didn't go weight training and I've not had spinach since school.

- **Keeping all flesh out of public sight**

FEELING the need to cover up whatever the weather and whatever the situation. I know it's 152 degrees outside and you're all in bikinis but I'm fine in my cardigan. Just fine. Not madly sweating at all. No. I'm perfectly happy, thank you.

- **Mirror horror**

FEELING horrified when you catch a glimpse of yourself as you pass a shop window or mirror. You glance sideways and see this fat woman looking back at you.

"She's waddling alongside me," you think. "What's she doing? She looks just like me, only she's about four stone heavier than me." Then – Oh shit – it is me. Damn.

- **The horror of a photograph**

STAGGERING BACKWARDS in disbelief when you see a photograph of yourself on holiday, or tagged by some helpful soul on Facebook. Yes, you know you're overweight, but not THAT overweight. Not, like, twice the size of everyone else in the picture.

- **Eating in public becomes really complicated**

WHEN YOU EAT, you feel judged. You feel as if every eye in the restaurant is on you as you choose which food you want (anything but salad and you feel you might shrivel up and die with the looks you are getting), then every eye is on you as you eat your food, and you wonder just how much of it you should actually consume, and how much you should leave on your plate so people think better of you.

Enjoying the meal and relishing the night out become secondary to trying to behave in a way which is 'appropriate' for your weight.

Spoiler alert – there is no 'appropriate' way to behave. Enjoy your night out and ignore everything but the food you are eating and the people you are sharing your evening with.

- **The looks people give you**

BEING fat is recognising a look in a stranger's eye as they wonder how on earth you got yourself into that state. Do you have no self-control? No pride in your appearance? It's easy to lose weight – just keep your mouth shut and don't eat so much. They don't say it, but you feel it, and that's what matters.

- **Being conscious of the sound you make**

EVERY LITTLE SOUND WORRIES YOU: how loud your footsteps are on wooden floors, worrying that the wonky floorboards creak much more when you step on them than when anyone else does. Stepping into the lift and feeling it groan a bit, and wondering whether anyone else noticed.

My friend loved to go rowing, and was very good at it, but she stopped because she hated the way the boat moved on the water as she got into it, and she became convinced that the others would rather she was no longer in their team. (She was wrong – they were all devastated when she left.)

- **Dreading a fat joke on TV or in a film**

You know that feeling when they are heading towards an offensive joke, or two characters nudge one another when a fat person walks in? Well, those moments are horrible, especially if you are in a group and you are the only person who is overweight. You feel torn about whether to throw the punchline in first, and get to the joke quicker than they do, leave the room, or groan at the obviousness of it all. I just sit there, scowling at the television in silence while doing all three of those things in my head.

SLIMMING CLUB: THE REAL STORY

You've had enough: you don't want to live like this anymore. It's all too much like hard work, so you sign up for a slimming club. Here are some of the things you can expect:

- The room you meet in won't be pleasant: it won't be a trendy bar or up-market restaurant. It will be a scruffy old community centre or church hall and you should count yourself lucky if it has carpet.
- On your first day you'll walk in and won't know where to go or what to do. People in the group will eye you suspiciously…especially if you are not very overweight. You'll see people discussing recipes, syns or points, green foods, red foods – it's all a new world with its own language and rules.

- If you look to one side you will see a long queue: this is people waiting, in various states of undress, to be weighed. Look carefully and you will notice that it is usually a TW (thin woman) doing the weighing, and NTWs (non-thin women) waiting to be weighed.
- Look more closely and you will notice something else about those in the queue… They will have removed everything bar the absolute essentials in order to get their weight down. You'll start week one wearing your shoes and coat, and by week six you'll be sporting nothing but your wedding ring and a thong.
- Everyone loses a lot of weight in the first week. This acts as a motivator so you come back the second week. But it is a cruel, cruel trick, because in the second week you will only lose a pound and you will collapse in desperation at the fact that you ate half as much and lost hardly anything, so you'll lose the plot and eat nothing but chocolate and chips, come back and discover you have lost 3 lbs. This will make you wonder whether, in fact, the key to weight loss is to ignore everything you are being told.
- You know when you go to the doctor and he asks you how much you drink? And even though you have had a bottle and a half of wine to yourself the night before, you will say, "Oh, just a couple of glasses of wine a week." Well, the food diary you are asked to keep will be just like that. You will report that you ate slivers of

grapefruit for breakfast, but forget to mention the milky coffee and croissants afterwards. You will mention the radish salad, but not the fish and chips, you won't remember the vodka and the kebab, but you will remember the squeeze of fresh lemon into a glass of water and the peeled grape. It's just that your memory isn't great...that's all. It's not that everyone makes the whole thing up: not at all.

- Most slimming groups have 'free foods' or 'green light' foods. That means you have to exert no control over yourself while eating them. They are free of guilt and don't need monitoring. The trouble is, you can make anything fattening, and though chicken and broccoli are on the 'free' lists, it turns out that covering them in batter and frying them, then dipping them in garlic mayonnaise before eating them, lifts them right off the free list and onto the top of the 'red list' of foods that one should never eat. You will only discover this simple error after putting on about a stone.
- You'll be told to cook everything by frying or roasting with a gentle spray of 'one calorie' cooking oil. The idea of adding just one calorie to foods when you cook is an appealing one, so you will adopt this strategy with gusto, but then you'll realise that in order to fry a small red onion you need to tip two whole bottles into the pan. About 500 calories, certainly way more

than if you'd just used a teaspoon of olive oil in the first place.

- A young man will join the group at some stage during your time there. He will come, be mothered by everyone, stay for a couple of weeks in which he will lose more weight than all the others put together, then never be seen again.

THE MYSTERY OF DISAPPEARING FAT

It's one of life's great mysteries... You lose weight; there's less fat on you. So, where is it? Where has it gone?

Is there a big fat store somewhere? Up on a cloud, or something?

Well, no. The rather dull answer to the question is that fat is converted to carbon dioxide and water. You exhale the carbon dioxide and the water mixes into your circulation until it's lost as urine or sweat. When you think about it like that, fat isn't such a big drama, is it?

To offer a little more detail: say you lose 10 kg of fat, precisely 8.4 kg comes out through your lungs as you breathe away the carbon dioxide, and the remaining 1.6 kg turns into water. In other words, nearly all the weight we lose is exhaled.

It's just air!

Almost everything we eat comes back out via the lungs.

Protein is pretty much the same except that a small percentage of it is lost in urine.

The only thing in food that makes it to your colon undigested is dietary fibre (things like corn which, without being too indelicate, stays whole and you can sometimes see it when you go to the toilet). Everything else you swallow is absorbed into your bloodstream and organs, and is then vaporised.

So, a little bit more science coming up. I hope this all makes sense because I think it's quite important to get a handle on the science, so you know what your body is doing. Let's take a person who is around eleven and a half stone (75 kg). Their resting metabolic rate (that's the rate at which the body uses energy when they aren't moving) produces about 590 grams of carbon dioxide per day. All the research shows that there is no pill or potion you can buy that will increase that figure, despite the bold claims you might have heard from caffeine pill manufacturers.

The good news is that you exhale 200 grams of carbon dioxide while you're fast asleep every night, so you've already breathed out a quarter of your daily target before you even step out of bed.

Maybe we all just need to breathe more?

It seems sensible to ask: if fat turns into carbon dioxide, should we all just be breathing a lot more...taking bigger breaths and breathing frantically after a big meal in order to lose weight? Sadly, that's not how it works: huffing and puffing more than you need will only make you dizzy.

The only way you can consciously increase the amount of carbon dioxide your body is producing is by moving your muscles more. In other words – exercising. Going for a walk triples your metabolic rate, and so will cooking, gardening, vacuuming and sweeping. You don't have to run marathons or lift heavy weights, you just need to move a bit, be more active.

That's why exercise is a useful part of a weight-loss programme.

POSITIVE THINKING

This isn't a woo-woo, think happy thoughts chapter, but a look at ways in which, if you're overweight and feeling low, you can try and make yourself feel better. Here are six tips for feeling happier, calmer and at one with the world. They come from readers who have contacted me through social media during the ten years I've been writing the Mary Brown.

1. Learn to accept the word 'fat'

Helen, Manchester

Helen writes that there are lots of ways of talking about people who are carrying a few extra pounds without ever using the word FAT. People are curvy, larger, plus-size, Rubenesque. People avoid the word fat. "But what is so terribly awful about the word? Why have we all attached such negativity to it? If someone refers to themselves as 'fat', don't tell them they're not, or offer other more palatable words. If we used the word without turning it into an offensive term, perhaps we would demystify it a bit."

People will have mixed views about this, but I have to say it resonates with me. When I set out to write a series of novels about someone who was overweight, I wanted them to be the sort of books that would be read by everyone because they were fun, lively and interesting. It didn't matter what size the heroine of the book was – she was a super character full of heart and mischief. But I also very much wanted to make her fat because there simply aren't enough amusing, complicated, witty, thought-provoking characters who are overweight.

What were people fearful of? The fat won't jump off my character's stomach and attack you! She's fat. There are reasons why she's fat. It's an important part of her character. It's not all of her character, not by a long way, but it's important nonetheless.

2. Learn to love your body

Sharon, Exeter

This is what we all need to do: no doubt about it. Whatever your size. You're only fat, not grotesque. Your body gets you from place to place, allows you to meet people, fall in love, possibly have children and enjoy all the lovely luxuries that life offers; from walks in the park, to lying down on the grass and snoozing in the afternoon sun. You can still walk, run, swim, dance and play, or sit in the garden and read a magazine. The only thing stopping you is your fears about what other people think. Stop worrying right now.

. . .

3. Remember that fad diets don't work

Michelle, Woking

Michelle is right: despite the allure of a quick-fix, we know deep down that drinking nothing but green liquid day-after-day, unless it's medically approved, will do us more harm than good. Sure, if you eat nothing but candle wax and rhubarb for the next six weeks, you will lose loads of weight, but you'll just put it back on when you revert to the way you had been eating.

Treat your body nicely. Nurture it with healthy food, exercise and fresh air.

If fad diets worked in the long-term, there would be no more need for them. But there always is. All the time. New diets, new food plans, new ways to lose weight that will do you way more damage as you yo-yo diet up and down the scales, than if you'd just stayed the same weight in the first place.

4. Ignore unsolicited advice about weight loss

Michael, Sunderland

Someone might come to you with the best motives in the world, and tell you all about how he or she lost weight, but you are not that person...you are you. You need to create your own weight-loss plan, one that works for you. Unless you particularly requested this person's input and value their thoughts, ignore them. Don't be confused or thrown off track by someone who tells you about their turnip and lemon peel diet, or that the sure-fire way to lose weight is to eat while standing on one leg.

5. Never tell someone that what they are wearing is 'flattering'

Marie, Cardiff

If you want to compliment a fat person on what they're wearing, avoid saying it's 'flattering'. 'Flattering' means, "Your clothes are hiding the bit of your body that society doesn't like." Just tell them they look great. Tell them they look lovely. Say "Wow." Tell them they look hot. Tell them they look good. Don't tell them that the outfit they are wearing looks good.

6. Be kind

Angela, Hounslow

I made a decision to treat my body with kindness and respect. It suddenly dawned on me that my body had carried my children and nourished them in the first days of their lives, cycled with them to school, worked hard, travelled, swam in the sea and coped with a lifetime of stresses and strains. So, it's overweight. So what? We're all different sizes and that's a good thing. And all those sizes should be equally valid.

SECTION THREE

WORK

THE STORIES

This is the tale of a 27-year-old woman called Catherine Baxter who worked as a receptionist at a veterinary surgery.

Catherine had been working at the surgery for around nine months and loved her job. She'd made friends with the other staff in the busy practice and had become particularly fond of working with the animals. The vets at the practice were full of praise for her and said they were delighted she'd joined them. They commented on how smart and efficient she was as well as being caring with the animals and sensitive to the pets' owners.

"I knew that this was the job for me, and I'd thought about ways in which I could progress my career, doing courses in animal welfare in the evenings, or animal management. I'd even considered doing animal psychology. In short – I was very happy, enjoying the daily interaction with the customers. I was the first person they saw when they came into the practice, and I knew how to reassure them, and put them at ease. I planned to stay there for a long time."

Things were going well in her life.

"In addition to the job being great, I had a fiancé and was busy planning our wedding, I lived in a sunny flat in a friendly neighbourhood, and had lots of friends close by. I thought I'd hit the jackpot.

"I was about a UK size 14 at the time (not that I'd considered that to be remotely relevant, but it came to be), and fairly fit and healthy. Life was good.

"But around Christmas time, some nine months after I'd joined the company, my fiancé announced that he no longer wanted to be with me. The news came completely out of the blue. I felt like I'd been shot when he told me. None of my friends could believe it either.

"He moved out of the flat straight after telling me, and the emptiness and loneliness I felt almost crushed me. I have to confess that I coped by eating and drinking. I'd lose myself in huge grab bags of tortilla chips and bottles of wine. Every time friends came round, we'd order pizza. Once the friends had gone, I'd finish all the pizza that was left and any other treats left lying around. I ate away the pain and misery. While I was eating, I wasn't thinking about what had happened. I came to look forward to food more than I looked forward to anything else in my life.

"I had to wear a uniform to work – kind of like a nurse's tunic and trousers to make us look smart and professional. Before long, the one I had was too tight for me, so I spoke to the office manager and ordered another. I asked whether I could keep hold of the uniform I had because I was definitely going to diet and fit back into it. She said that was fine.

"Then I discovered that the reason my fiancé had split up with me was because he'd met someone else – someone tall, skinny and blonde. I couldn't resist torturing myself by looking at pictures of them on social media. The two of them on holiday, at parties (with people who I considered friends) and staring into one another's eyes. God it was nauseating. It was also extremely painful, and I coped with it all by eating even more.

"It wasn't long before the larger uniform was skin-tight. Bulges appeared and the buttons at the front gaped. I hadn't been to the gym in months and was aware that I was waddling a little. It seemed to happen so quickly. Within four months I had put on a good couple of stone, and was in an XL uniform. I was told that was the biggest pair of trousers they had in stock.

"I mumbled something about losing weight and Jen, the only female vet at the practice, said she thought that would be a good idea. I went to the loos and burst into tears."

At a team meeting later that day it was suggested that Catherine should work behind the scenes, as an assistant, rather than on the front desk where she was the 'face' of the company.

"I didn't think anything of it at first, until Sue, the other receptionist, said she'd overheard them talking, and that I wasn't a good image for the company now I'd put on so much weight. I got really upset when I heard this. I loved the interaction with the customers, and I knew the new role would be as dogsbody. Then I felt cross: my fiancé had caused all this. My life was spiralling out of control because of him and he was off gallivanting around the place with his new girlfriend.

"So, I ate more. I never addressed the demotion with my bosses because I was too embarrassed to bring up the issue, but I know why they did it. These days I just bring the hay in from outside and act as a gofer. I feel a bit hopeless really. I guess if I got a grip and lost weight, they would put me back in the customer services role, but why should I? What has my weight got to do with anything? I bet this would never happen to a man. People have a vision of what a competent, professional woman looks like, and being fat isn't part of the package. I don't enjoy the new position anywhere near as much as the old one, and am thinking of leaving. I can't believe how much my life has changed because I put on weight. It doesn't seem fair."

What do you make of that? The story was told to me by a woman responding to a survey I conducted for this book. We'll come on to the results of the survey later, but what was really interesting was that lots of people who filled in the questionnaire, also sent through stories of how they thought their weight had had an impact at work. In every case, the person being discriminated against because of their weight, felt it was their fault, or felt too ashamed/embarrassed to challenge the decision, because they found it demeaning to have to discuss their weight with their bosses, so they just acquiesced.

The one person who did challenge her bosses couldn't prove that it was because of her weight. She put on weight and was moved to a backroom role with the company, but couldn't prove that she was moved to a backroom role because she put on weight, so when she challenged it, they denied they'd changed her job because of her weight. It's extremely difficult.

But there can be no question, surely, that changing someone's job, against their will, because they put on weight, is, plain discrimination. Could you do that to someone with a disability or illness? Could you do it to someone of colour? Is it any less discriminatory to take action against someone because they are fat?

Why the judgements?

One interesting thing to ponder in all this is: why do people judge someone who is overweight as being 'less than' someone who is thin? In this example, Catherine was clearly seen as being less attractive/ professional/approachable when she had put on weight.

Is weight really that big a deal? Do you think anyone would be put off buying something if the person they were dealing with was fat? Especially when it's a veterinary surgery. Surely the only thing you're worrying about is your pet, and making sure they are as well as possible, not whether the assistant is a size 14 or a size 18?

And what if you put on weight through medication? What if it's not your fault? I went on a trip to South America a few years ago, and was bitten by an insect. By the time I returned home, my arm had swelled to twice its normal size and I felt very ill. I went to hospital and was given a steroid injection, and was kept in hospital for a week while the infection settled, then put on steroids.

The pain disappeared and the swelling went down, but after a few months on steroids my weight had gone nuts. I was getting bigger at an alarming rate and there was nothing I could do about it. My face looked like a puffer fish and none of my clothes fitted.

Should this change in appearance have led to my bosses moving me to a new role? I would have been horrified if it had. Surely if you do a job which doesn't rely on your appearance, and for which a certain appearance is not a requisite, then to penalise you because of your appearance is plain discrimination.

But it's very hard to prove discrimination unless they tell you that your weight is the problem. How can you possibly prove it, if they deny that was the reason? A lengthy court case? It is also the case that the brutal reality of life at work means the tiny discriminations that can pop up through the day can be hard to spot as they happen, which makes challenging them when they come to a head very hard.

Our perceptions and idealised notions of what makes a successful businesswoman, are based on our belief that thinness means success. Think of a businesswoman in your mind… You think of someone slim, probably in a pencil skirt, sitting on a large desk, slender legs crossed in front of her. You think of the glamorous women who are successful in shows like: *Suits, The Good Wife, House of Cards*. How many fat women are there in them? Is it true that no one in business is over a size zero? Of course not, but if you watch these shows you could believe that. Some are blonde, some brunette, others are redheads. The one thing they have in common is that they are slim.

More worrying than the idealised Hollywood images of women in work as thin, are actual examples of organisations who now state that they prefer to employ people who are thin.

Victoria Hospital in Texas is explicit about it. They say they won't hire anyone with a body mass index of more than 35 (about 15 and a half stone, or 220 pounds for someone who is 5 foot 6).

In 2015, a solicitor's firm called Crossland Employment Solicitors conducted a survey of 1,000 companies (in the UK) and their attitudes to overweight employees. The results were illuminating.

The results showed that companies felt that people who were overweight were seen as being less likely to be productive, and were less likely to be hired for jobs.

Nearly half of the companies spoken to said they would be less inclined to recruit an applicant at interview stage if they were obese.

"On the face of it, the odds are against you getting a job if you are overweight," said Beverley Sunderland, managing director at Crossland.

It's pretty scary stuff.

This is especially worrying in light of the European Court of Justice's ruling in 2014 that obesity may be a disability if it causes a long-term impairment that prevents the employee from doing their job at the same level as other workers.

The ruling means that employers now have to find ways to accommodate obese workers who fall within this definition of disability. If an obese person tells an employer about their long-term conditions at interview and the company does not employ them, the applicant could try and claim disability discrimination, lawyers say.

Considering that a quarter of people in the UK are obese, it's shocking that discrimination takes place. But, there's no doubt that it does. In 2019, Pakistan International Airlines was reported to have explained to the overweight cabin crew that if they didn't lose weight, they wouldn't be able to fly.

So, in short, overweight people are less likely to be hired, are lower paid, and have fewer opportunities. It is women who bear the brunt of this prejudice. Before getting into the detail of why it happens and what can be done about it, let's move onto the survey I conducted to test whether issues like these occurred in the UK.

THE SURVEY

I decided to conduct a survey about the issues facing overweight people at work. So, in July 2019 I carried out a research project through social media. I have to say that the results were shocking. I had expected there to be some examples of people who'd felt as if they were treated differently because they were overweight, but I didn't expect anything like the feedback I received. Loads of people answered five simple questions, and many of them followed up by contacting me separately with their stories (these follow as case studies in the next chapter). I don't claim that this is a highly scientific survey but it's a snapshot of how overweight people feel about getting jobs and working.

The results combined to paint a very dim view of the world of work for those who are overweight.

These answers were given by 652 people who self-identified themselves as either overweight or obese.

. . .

QUESTION ONE: Do you think your weight has ever prevented you from getting a job?

YES: 568

NO: 0

DON'T KNOW: 84 (i.e.: they had not applied for a job since putting on weight, didn't work or simply didn't know whether their weight had ever had an impact)

WHAT WAS interesting about these figures, to me, was that no one answered 'no'. Not one person could say with certainty that their weight had never been an issue when they were applying for jobs. It's shocking, and very sad. Obviously, it's impossible to know whether their weight was any factor at all. This survey can only measure the respondents' feelings. Still, I think it provides an important measure of just how lousy overweight people feel, and how much they feel it is affecting them in everyday life.

It's shocking. But once you start looking at other surveys, it seems that my results are not so surprising after all.

In 2018, psychologist Stuart W. Flint, of Sheffield Hallam University, conducted a survey in which the participants were given hypothetical CVs with photographs of fat and thin people. They were asked to select which of the candidates they'd be likely to choose to come and work for them. They chose the ones who were of average weight to be the most suitable. Obese women were the least likely to be hired because they were seen as lazy and less physically able.

Then, in 2019, researchers in the USA (University of Pennsylvania) conducted similar experiments and found that obese people were not picked because they were seen to be "lazy, incompetent, unattractive, lacking willpower".

QUESTION TWO: Do you think your weight has ever had an impact on your earnings?

YES: 305

NO: 185

Don't know: 162

THIS RESULT WAS MUCH CLOSER, I'm relieved to say, but there was a high number of people who opted for 'don't know' as the answer to the question. It's very hard, if you work in an organisation without a transparent wage structure, to know what other people are earning, let alone why differences might exist. It can be hard to compare jobs, and it can be difficult to know in your own mind why people are paid what they are paid.

Despite all this, almost half the people who answered the question thought that their income had been adversely affected by their weight.

Again, this is something that other researchers have found. In 2016, University of Exeter research concluded that an extra stone in weight could cost a woman £1,500 a year. They took comparable women and concluded that a woman who was a stone heavier would on average earn £1,500 less, compared to a woman of the same height in a similar (comparable) role. And the inequality doesn't end there. Overweight people also worked longer hours and were found to be considered less qualified for leadership positions. The research states that they were expected to be less successful.

In an earlier study, in 2014, researchers at Vanderbilt University in Nashville discovered that women who were overweight earned less money than slimmer women, whereas obese men seem to do just as well as slim men. This led researcher Jennifer Shinall to say: "It really seems to be more of a sex-discrimination issue."

Tam Fry of the Obesity Forum agrees: "Overweight women suffer far more than overweight men." This is, presumably, because people think women should be slim and attractive, so more judgement is cast onto those who aren't. In contrast, people don't judge men on their appearance quite so much, so if they are overweight, it is not seen to be an indication of their ability to do a job. And the thing is – it isn't an indication of how well they can do their job, so that's fair enough, but neither is it an indication of how a woman will perform in a job, but she is judged regardless. And that's where the problem lies. "I have interviewed many overweight people who have been victimised in one way or another – and the majority of them were women," adds Fry.

Question THREE: Do you think your weight has affected your chances when the company selects people to represent it in a public role?

YES: 429

NO: 0

Don't know: 223

THIS QUESTION WAS DESIGNED to see whether respondents felt that, though they may be gainfully employed and not actively discriminated against on a daily basis, when it came to more public roles, they were overlooked. So, when it came to public speaking, giving lectures or being 'front of house', did they notice a difference in the way they were treated? Many did!

I asked this question because in many of the sections in this book, the women I spoke to felt they were tolerated rather than promoted. Women who felt their boyfriends were loving when they were at home together, but didn't want to be seen in public with them. Clothes shops who discouraged fat people, and restaurants who seated the overweight in the darker recesses of the restaurant instead of in the window seats. I wondered whether it was the same at work, and it seems it was.

Author, Roxane Gay, wrote a memoir in which she described the painful situations she encountered as an obese woman. She recalls the organisers of literary events being embarrassed by her appearance. They were surprised, Gay felt, that a writer with a degree of success and public acclaim, could be so overweight. It was as if they thought the two went hand-in-hand: success and thinness. Which, by extension must mean there were assumptions that now she was revealed to be overweight, she could not be considered as successful. Which is plainly absurd.

People cared about her weight when she stood in front

of them and spoke, but not when she was quietly, behind the scenes, writing away. They loved her books and wanted her physical appearance to tie in with their expectations of what a successful novelist should look like.

Gay was clear about how much these reactions hurt: they illustrated to her how little people thought of fat people, and how people assumed the overweight were neither smart nor capable.

Studies routinely find it is overweight *women* who bear the brunt of this disrespect and discrimination, and are discouraged from taking on public/visible roles.

Susie Orbach, the author of *Bodies* and *Fat is a Feminist Issue,* explains: "Historically, the notion of a big guy has always been perfectly acceptable. Men are meant to be big and strong, and women are meant to be tiny and not take up too much space. They can have everything in the world now, but they have to be slim. That's the horror of the current aesthetics for women. Young girls are taught at an early age that their bodies are for display and not for anything else."

This is not to suggest that all overweight women suffer at work, or that no overweight men do. Some people have more enlightened bosses than others. But all the research I have looked at indicates that it is a widespread problem.

QUESTION FOUR: Have you suffered from bullying at work because of your weight? (Bullying to include name calling, comments and mimicking/mocking behaviour)

YES: 476
NO: 70
Don't know: 106

THIS WAS the most difficult question for people to answer. I had more queries about it than any of the other questions. For some people, going to work is traumatic due to the bullying they experience there.

A saleswoman in a British clothes shop wrote that she had been forced to walk out in front of customers in a uniform that was too small while her managers looked her up and down. A male employee who gained weight was told by his manager to utilise the company gym because she was unhappy about him being 'plus-size'.

Others declined to be interviewed. One woman commented: "I am never going to share my story. It has cost me years to get over it." Another wrote: "I suspect my story about discrimination will have the opposite effect. Fat people are hardly ever depicted in the media as successful. Our heads are cut off from photographs. That's why dehumanising incidents in the workplace are no surprise."

Her conclusion is bleak: "As long as we are all terrified of becoming fat, this will go on. Yes, we are terrified. Because we all know how fat people are treated in this society."

According to Orbach, "Large people are demonised because we have a widespread panic about bodies and food. Lots of people who are so-called normal weight struggle with eating problems … [but] the thing about larger people is that their problems show, and nobody wants to know. What we project on larger people are aspects of ourselves that we are trying to hide from."

Fry says such prejudice against overweight people can easily lead to outright bullying at work. "For some people, it is horrific to go to work because of the bullying they can expect when they get there. This kind of bullying is particularly shameful because their weight may be beyond their control. There are many fat people who have a genetic or metabolic disposition to being fat."

QUESTION FIVE: In your opinion, has your weight had an impact on your career development?

YES: 420
NO: 13
Don't know: 219

A FAMILIAR PATTERN IS EMERGING. Very few 'no's. Most of those who answered the survey questions failed to rule out whether their weight played a part in their career development (i.e.: how much progress they made once in a job, as distinct from whether they actually got the job in the first place). Nearly 65% said 'yes' – they thought being overweight had affected their career development. In other words – most people by quite a long way.

Is that shocking? It certainly seems so to me: it also seems utterly nonsensical. On what planet is it OK to stop someone from developing in their job for any reason other than lack of ability? You offer promotions to the best people; not the thinnest. To do so is not just egregious in the extreme, but it's not professional and can only harm your business. Insanity. It would make as much sense to penalise those who wear blue shoes, or carry brown handbags.

So, what does all this mean?

There is no doubt that a woman's weight has a significant impact on her earnings. There have been hundreds of studies and they all reach the same conclusion: women who are overweight earn less.

One study by Professor Mark Roehling (Michigan State University) and Professor Patricia Roehling (Hope College) concluded: "Weight bias may contribute to the glass ceiling on the advancement of women to the top levels of management." That study estimated that overweight women earned between $9,000 and $19,000 less than their 'average' weight counterparts.

Additionally, they found that only 5% of male and female CEOs at top US companies were obese with a body mass index (BMI) over 30. This is much lower than the US average percentage of obese men and women, which is currently at 36% (men) and 38% (women) for the same age group.

However, the most shocking study finding was the difference between male and female CEOs when the parameters are widened to include those who are overweight. The survey found that between 45% and 61% of top male CEOs were overweight but only 5% of top female CEOs were overweight. Their view was: "This suggests greater tolerance for a larger size among men but not women."

Sadly, this study finding of weight discrimination against women in business doesn't appear to be limited to the United States. My simple study echoes all the findings of the American researchers.

What it means, in short, is that women wanting to advance into the highest levels of business management have to take into consideration the fact that society places stricter weight standards on women than men.

It also means women around the world need to work together to help employers and hiring managers become aware of and overcome ingrained biases of how people's weight affects hiring and promotion decisions.

And one of the most frightening things in this is that it seems to be getting worse. The media ideal of what a 'normal female' looks like is thinner today than ever. Whether you're looking at female cartoon characters, movie/television actresses, *Playboy* centrefolds or beauty contest winners, they have all become thinner over the decades.

I think it's worth looking at one final study in this section, because the work of Timothy A. Judge, from the University of Florida, and Daniel M. Cable, from the London Business School, is very good, and very relevant. They set out to test the norms that society holds with regards to body standards for men versus women. They examined what they called "the relationship between weight and income and the degree to which the relationship varies by gender".

Here are some of their findings:

- Gaining weight is more damaging to women's earnings than to men's.
- Whereas women are punished for any weight gain, very thin women receive the most severe punishment for their first few pounds of weight gain, because thinness is seen as being central to female attractiveness.
- 'Very thin' women earn approximately $22,000 more than their average weight counterparts.
- 'Thin' women earn a little over $7,000 more than their average weight counterparts.

What does this study tell us? It shows us that, as a society, our physical appearance plays a key role in workplace interactions and earnings outcomes. It shows us that many employers and hiring agents have ingrained biases.

THE CASE STUDIES

Many respondents to the survey also chose to include their own personal stories to illustrate the problems they had been facing. I thought it was worth sharing some of those here because they illustrate, perhaps more powerfully than the numbers, how destructive 'fat shaming' discrimination can be.

One of the people who responded was Margaret who worked at a temping recruitment agency. Her story came alongside the third question (please note: all names have been changed):

Do you think your weight has affected your chances when the company selects people to represent it in a public role?

"Yes, I do! I was very good at my job, but I was never invited to external meetings or to go out and meet clients. Not ever. Other people of my level were, and people on the rung below me, but not me. I was the only one who was fat. I don't want to leap to unfair conclusions, I'm really not paranoid or anything, but it felt to me like they were hiding me away.

"Lots of external meetings took place with companies that were looking to recruit temps, and they never wanted me to go to them. They would let me talk to the temps who came into the office, and they kept telling me how good I was on the phone but I always felt they were keeping me away from the big, important clients. At first, I thought I just needed to build my professional reputation, but then someone who was younger and less experienced than me was sent out to meetings. I couldn't work out what it was, and worried a lot about the fact that they didn't really rate me."

But then Margaret started to lose weight. She lost around a stone at first, then began a fitness campaign and lost more weight, eventually going down from a size 18 to a size 12.

She wrote in her note that soon after she lost weight she was asked to go to external meetings, and was invited to give talks and go to client lunches. She went to board presentations and her stock in the company grew, leading to more opportunities, promotions and pay rises. She'd always thought it was because she gained so much confidence after losing weight, and that people could see she was ready for new challenges. "But then one of my colleagues was brutally honest with me. He said it was nothing to do with my confidence, it was because when I was fat, they didn't think I was the right image for the company externally. They didn't want to send a fat person out in their name."

Another woman who wrote in with her story was Janet, a teacher. She responded to the fourth question:

Have you suffered from bullying at work because of your weight? (Bullying to include name calling, comments and mimicking/mocking behaviour)

She complained about being called names at work, and having to cope with being referred to as 'the whale' and 'blubber mountain'. Not from students, as you might expect, but from fellow teachers.

Janet wrote: "Another staff member is homosexual and he once told me how hard it had been for him to be accepted. I said: it's been like that for me too, because I am fat. The guy looked at me, horrified for a moment, then nodded and agreed that he had seen what a tough time I'd been given."

Janet said the bullying was so bad that she felt as if her job was at risk. "The deputy head said that I would be dismissed because I lost a test form – this simply cannot be a reason to dismiss a person. I think the real reason is that she feels my body is an embarrassment to the school. She doesn't want parents to be confronted with an obese teacher."

Janet thought about what to do about the situation, but the comments and the digs were so underhand that it was hard for her to prove she was being discriminated against because of her weight.

Fat-shaming/bullying is a real problem, and it is the unseen discrimination that is hardest to deal with, as it can always be denied. Unconscious bias is very hard too. It means that people are speaking down to you and insulting you without realising they are doing it.

"We grow up believing that fat people are unhealthy and have no self-control. As if they are somehow choosing to be overweight. Who would choose to be overweight? It's one thing to get on with life and be happy whatever your size, but another to go out and actively choose obesity," said Janet.

People are overweight for a variety of reasons – medication, thyroid issues, emotional issues with food and addiction.

Anna wrote in after reading the fifth question:

In your opinion, has your weight had an impact on your career development?

She said she had wanted to speak out at work many times when she felt like she was being treated differently because of her weight, but she couldn't do it. She concluded:

"I didn't feel comfortable talking about the shaming that goes on. Sometimes it really hurts but no one's doing it on purpose. How do you stop people doing something they are not doing on purpose? And it's all the little things... They all go out and look round the shops at lunchtime, but never invite me because – why would they? – I can't fit into the clothes in Topshop and New Look. So, I'm slightly apart from the rest of the group... I don't go to the gym with them or any of the classes. They are nice to me but they don't invite me anywhere or chat to me about their boyfriends, or parties or anything. I know it's not *because* I'm fat, but it kind of is. They treat me differently because of my weight. It makes me feel so anxious and as if I shouldn't be there...as if I'm not welcome there."

A survey conducted by researchers at a university in Virginia concluded that over half of Americans had no qualms about making negative comments about a person's weight.

Such surveys along with a growing feeling in America that fat-shaming is the only shaming that it is now acceptable, have led to a new push for change. Leading this push is the Fat Acceptance Movement who want new laws to tackle the bias in social attitudes. This movement has its critics: people argue that it minimises the problem of obesity in America. But many public health researchers argue that it's the body shaming that's making things worse, not better.

Peggy Howell, a spokeswoman at the National Association to Advance Fat Acceptance, says she got involved with the movement after her boss threatened to fire her from her job as a school counsellor if she didn't lose weight. "He believed that if I couldn't control my weight, then my life was out of control and I had no business being a counsellor to others who needed help," she says.

Some of the stories I heard during the research were quite horrible and hinted at deliberate discrimination, others were simply sad. They are all unacceptable, but as all respondents said, it's hard to call it out. It's hard to stand up and say: "You are mocking me because I am fat," because you have to publicly acknowledge that you are overweight, and that's difficult. So, what do you do? The next chapter offers some practical responses.

FINDING SOLUTIONS

It's all very well and good moaning about how unfair life is, but that's not going to change things. This chapter looks at what you can actually do to address grievances when you feel your weight has had a negative impact on your ability to succeed and thrive at work. I hope you find the following seven suggestions helpful.

1. Write it down

Every time someone behaves in a way that offends you or upsets you: write it down and email it to yourself. Keep a file of emails from yourself, written contemporaneously, that show the problems you are dealing with. It will be hard to remember each individual incident in six months' time if it comes to a head, you'll need to have it written down.

. . .

2. Find an advocate

Can you find an advocate or defender in the office? If you confide in someone in the office and talk to them on a human level about just how much this is affecting you, and how much you feel it is damaging your career, it might help. Then if any gossiping takes place when you're not there, they might step in on your behalf and mention lightly how much their attitude upsets you. Things won't change overnight, but it will start a slow process of people being more cautious when they talk about you.

3. Complain to HR

The obvious step to take if you want to sort out the problem formally.

4. Talk to an employment lawyer

A decent lawyer will speak to you free of charge before you engage him, and will give you the advice you need.

5. Find another job

Leave and get a job somewhere else, and make it clear why you are leaving. It will help your mental health to be away from the place and if you make it clear why you are going, it might help those coming up behind you.

6. Confront the perpetrator outright

Obviously, it would be wise to do this calmly and

without resorting to shouting or abuse. But if you calmly confront the perpetrator you might find they had no idea of the impact of their words or deeds and may stop when it's brought to their attention.

7. Joke about it

To be honest, I'm not sure about this... It can be a tough thing to do, but in the same way that a comedian will mock anything about themselves that makes them stand out from the crowd as soon as they get on stage (Rob Beckett and his teeth, Greg Davies and his height), it can be very disarming.

It takes a lot of confidence, but if you're giving a presentation and open with: "My job is so stressful – when I started a few days ago I was a size eight and look at me now," people will warm to you. Beware though, it may give the impression that you are very comfortable with jokes being told about your weight.

SECTION FOUR

SUMMER

SUMMER JOYS, PART ONE

Let joy be unconfined, let there be dancing in the streets: the warm weather is finally here. After months of bone-shakingly cold mornings, having to de-ice the car every day and drive through grey rain to get to work, suddenly winter is fading away and, like a caterpillar turning into a bright and beautiful butterfly, spring is emerging from winter's chrysalis.

Flowers appear, the garden is bathed in dappled sunshine, and everything feels wonderful. You skip out to your (ice-free) car, and drive along while the blue, cloudless skies float merrily above you.

Spring is lovely.

The only problem with spring is that it leads to… SUMMER! Yes, all too soon, the gentle glow of spring is replaced by the fiery heat of summer. Leaving the house becomes like taking a journey into the depths of hell. You are wet all the time and people expect you to ditch your cardigan and let your bingo wings flap freely for all to see.

Summer is evil.

Oh yes, my friends, you know it's true. Advertisers will have us believe that summer is the season of tanned legs peeking from crisp, white cotton dresses, of smiley picnics and ice-creams but it is not. Don't listen to them. Ignore the TV images of pretty people laughing as they run upon golden sands.

Every fat person knows that summer is a vicious ride through a bubbling volcano. It's full of sweating, chafing, swollen hands and feet, and trying to cover up when the world around you is packed full of people who are stripping off.

Summer is sent down to earth to taunt and infuriate us and send us spiralling into an infernal battle between revealing flesh which promptly burns, and staying so covered up that you are quietly boiling to death.

It's awful. And you know what the really terrible thing is? It happens every damn year.

So, here is your indispensable guide to what the summer holds in store if you're carrying a couple of extra pounds (or three and a half tons in my case). Ignore the summer brochures full of thin, tanned people doing yoga in leotards on the beach at dusk, or dancing around in the sea with a concave stomach. This is the REAL guide to summer

Sweat

Let's start with sweat. I know – I'm sorry – it's not a pleasant conversation to have, but you're among friends here: so, I'll ask the question: just how much sweat can one person produce? How much? I don't understand why there is anything left of me when there's this much sweat pouring off me? I'm wet all the time.

Let me tell you how my day goes:

My sheets are soaking wet when I wake up in the mornings and I'm tangled up in them with damp hair which stands up on end when I run my hands through it. I look ridiculous. Young children would run and hide if they saw me walking zombie-like across the landing.

Next, I go into the shower and wash until I'm squeaky clean. I come back to the bedroom, towel dry and style my hair, then before I can even get my goddamned clothes on, I'm all sweaty again. Can this be right? I mean – how am I ever going to get dry? I stand in front of the fan to cool off, then get dressed as quickly as I can, but I have damp patches at the back of my neck and in my armpits before I get out of the house. Frankly, I look like I need another shower.

Next, the train to work. Oh, but this is the greatest joy of summer, isn't it? Public transport. What a thrill.

I stand on the train and feel the sweat running down my body under my blouse. I flap my arms like a chicken to try and cool it down, in the hope that I won't end up with enormous sweat patches. But it doesn't help, and people start looking at me like I've lost my mind, so I stop the chicken impressions and feel a long line of sweat slide down my back. Meanwhile, my make-up has practically slid off my face as I frantically dab at it to stop the sweat from running from my hairline into my eyes.

Then, someone stands up. Excellent. I can have a seat. Perhaps if I'm not struggling to balance, and staggering around in the aisle, I'll sweat less. Nope. This turns out not to be the case. I feel the sweat that was running down my back, still running. It is now pooling at the bottom of my back, and bottom. My thighs have stuck together, and still the sweat runs down my face. I probably look like Alice Cooper by now.

We're at my stop. Thank God. I stand up slowly and leave a little pool of myself behind, while my legs emit a loud farting sound as they peel off the seat. All this before I have made it to work.

There's no escaping the fact you will sweat when it's hot, so you may as well just embrace it, it is your body's way of regulating your temperature. Sweating has an important health role as it helps keep us cool, and – despite what you might think – sweat doesn't actually smell. It's only when it is mixed with bacteria on our skin that it starts to give off that pungent body odour scent. Admittedly it's not pleasant. The feeling of sweat running down your back inside your favourite silk blouse is a complete horror, but you've got to just ride it out. Buy cotton, wear loose clothing and try not to worry too much. We're all suffering as much as one another.

Clothing

What the hell do you wear when the sun is beaming down on you? Clearly, in the interests of staying cool, lighter garments are preferred, so it's off with the reliable woolly cardigan and on with a cotton or linen dress. But if it's fitted, and you're carrying a few extra pounds, you'll feel really uncomfortable all day. But then again, if it's too loose, you will look as if the dress is wearing you, as your head pops up through the middle of what looks like a tent. You need to cover the tops of your arms or you'll feel really self-conscious, but the only way to get cool is a fresh breath of air circulating around you. In short – summer is hard when it comes to dressing. You're better off going out naked, then you'll get arrested and thrown in a police cell and hopefully it will be nice and cool.

Feet

Did you know your feet put on weight? I was quite horrified to hear this. I thought feet were the one thing that didn't grow as you put on weight. But they do. So, by putting on weight and losing weight, you may find you have a shoe collection in which half of them don't fit you at any one time. Add to that the fact that feet can swell in the summer, and you have to look after them a little more in the hotter months of the year.

Obviously, a pedicure is a nice idea if you can afford one. Sitting back while someone massages, files, scrapes and oils your feet is one of the world's greatest feelings. If you don't fancy that, or if it's out of your price range, it might be worth buying a file from the chemists and some cooling gel and give your feet a mini pedicure at home after a bath or shower.

When it comes to shoes, it's not rocket science, really, is it – you need shoes in natural materials that allow your feet to breath (I hate writing that... I picture these feet with mouths on, desperately gasping for breath). Make sure your shoes fit properly, even when your feet swell, or you'll end up with blisters and sore feet for days. And no one wants to be a weird, sweaty fat person, hobbling along in a thick cardigan and ill-fitting shoes (see –

combined the first three points in one neat sentence there).

An unfortunate side-effect of getting too hot is swelling – and your ankles seem to cop the brunt of it. When we are hot our blood vessels expand to allow the blood to flow closer to the surface of the skin. This is our body's way of cooling our blood down. But, naturally, if our blood vessels expand, so do other areas of the body (stop sniggering at the back). As your ankles, and feet, are supporting your weight all day and have very little fat and muscle between the skin and blood vessels, you may notice them swelling more than other areas. The heat also causes our body to try and hold onto as much fluid as it can to prevent dehydration. Fluid retention tends to be more visible in smaller areas like your ankles.

SUMMER JOYS, PART TWO

The chafe

You were wondering when I was going to get to this, weren't you? I thought I'd build things up slowly, but there's no doubt that the prize for the very worst of all the summer pains is thigh chafe. Oh my God. Your thighs sting like a thousand bees have crawled down your leggings and it looks like your inner thighs have been boiled.

If you dare wear a dress without cycling shorts, anti-chafe cream or a reapplication of talcum powder every five minutes, you're in big trouble. Fat skin rubbing up against fat skin can be so painful you'll end up walking as though you've been riding a horse for the last three days. The site of the chafe often looks like it's been through a nasty burn incident. It's painful, and embarrassing and God it hurts.

Look out for the new shorts/leggings and accessories designed to beat it. Don't fight it. In a fight between woman and chafe, chafe will win every time.

. . .

Skin exposure

We live in a society where it's really not cool to be fat – it's seen as lazy and indulgent and deliberate. Fat people are still ritually mocked in stand-up comedy (as mentioned) and across the internet in hurtful memes.

It takes a lot of strength and guts to go out in summer as a fat person and wear what you want – to be unconcerned with showing the cellulite on your legs or arms, to show the stretch marks and fat rolls on your stomach when you dress in a crop top. But I think that's the only way to be. To cover up effectively would involve no sunbathing, no swimming in the sea, no summer dresses, flip flops, sandals or swimming costumes. The only way to cope would be to hide away til winter, and that's definitely not the right option to take.

Loneliness

I don't want to make this all too dark and desperate. But the fact is – given all that summer offers fat people – many women will stay in and withdraw from social activity instead of socialising. If you're invited to a pool party and you're much bigger than everyone else, it can feel really awkward, and you may be tempted to stay at home, alone. Summer then becomes a time of great isolation – a time when you feel you can't be outside without being judged, a time when you're worried about everything, a time when depression creeps in and darkens days that are carefree and happy for most other people.

This is to urge you not to isolate yourself indoors. Please get out and enjoy the sun on your beautiful face. Catch up with friends and enjoy the outdoors when you can. It'll soon be cold again; please try to emerge from your cocoon and enjoy it all when you can.

Swimming costumes

Oh, the awful angst of finding a swimming costume that doesn't look exactly like the one your nanna wore in the mid-1970s (and in her mid-70s). Can I not find some simple, straightforward, flattering costumes in elegant shapes and large sizes? I don't want a little skirt attached or a wild floral pattern. I just want a simple swimsuit in a choice of colours, much like the range of swimsuits that everyone else gets to choose from. I'll buy a kaftan if I want to cover up, all I want from you is a nice comfortable swimsuit without flowers, cherries or frills.

The beach

This is a tough arena. A place littered with obstacles: teeny tiny bikinis, staring, pointing children, and discomfort. And the day always ends in a red nose and sand in uncomfortable places. But it's also a great equaliser. People aren't really looking and judging, they are way too worried about being looked at and judged. The beach is somewhere you should be able to relax, catch the sun and cool down in the sea. What other people think is nothing to do with you. If they haven't got anything better to do than stare at you, you should be pitying them, not worrying about being judged by them.

SECTION FIVE

RELATIONSHIPS

DATING

Around 20 years ago (God, that makes me sound old), I met a guy called John who seemed to have it all – he was handsome, sophisticated, kind and funny. His family were lovely and he was intelligent and career-driven. I was working as a magazine journalist; I was in my 20s and a size 8. It felt like we were the perfect match. We went out on a series of dates to restaurants and theatres. We talked about the fact that we both used to go to a pub called the Red Lion, and remarked on how odd it was that we hadn't bumped into one another in there.

Then, one night after dinner, I suggested we should go there. We both knew the owners and had lots of friends who still went there. It would be good fun. John wasn't quite so sure, but I persuaded him, and we jumped into a cab.

Once we arrived, I strode up the stone steps outside and went to embrace the landlady. She smiled, hugged me and said how pleased she was to see me.

"Come in, come in," she said, wrapping her arm around me and leading me inside.

"John's here too," I said, indicating my boyfriend.

She glanced up, took one look at him and pulled her arm from around my shoulder.

"He's not coming in," she said.

"Why not?"

"He's just not."

I wasn't going to go in without him, so John and I left to go to a nearby pub instead.

"Why wouldn't she let you in?" I asked.

"Oh, because of a thing that happened a while ago. It was nothing."

"Go on, tell me," I said.

"I had sex with her friend," he said.

"OK," I replied. "And – what? – you didn't call her or something?"

"No, I didn't take her number. I mean – I didn't know her name or anything."

"If you like someone enough to sleep with them, surely you like them enough to remember their name?" I said. But – in all honesty – I still didn't understand why his appearance had caused such a hostile reaction from the landlady. Sure, she might want to comment on his behaviour all those years ago, but to bar him completely seemed draconian.

"It wasn't about liking her enough to sleep with her," he said. "I was with her precisely because she was ugly. It was part of a game."

"What game?"

"It was the 'pull a pig' game – all of the guys in the pub

were playing it. I managed to sleep with the fattest person there, so I won."

"Christ," I said. Now I understood why he'd been barred. What a vile thing to do. And note the words he used – he was playing a game in which he had to have sex with the ugliest person, so he slept with the fattest person. Those two words were one and the same thing in his mind.

My relationship with John didn't last much longer, as you can imagine. But the story has stayed with me all these years. At the time, I remember thinking of the callousness of the man and how vile his behaviour was. Now I think more of the hurt and pain caused to the woman. She did nothing wrong. She went to a bar one evening because she was friends with the landlady, and she met what she thought was a nice, handsome man. Should she have thought straight away, "What if this is a joke? What if they are all taking the piss out of me?"

Absolutely not. The process of dating is complicated enough without having to worry that someone is taking the mickey out of you. But it does throw up lots of questions: regardless of your weight, how do you ever know whether a suitor is serious? How do you prevent yourself from being part of some cruel hoax? Is it any wonder that people (or should I change that to 'women' because I've yet to hear of a group of females playing 'pull the pig') are cautious about dating?

I thought about the story of my ex-boyfriend recently when I read Sophie Stevenson's story. In case you didn't hear the horrible tale, 24-year-old Sophie went on holiday to Barcelona with her friends, and while she was there, she met a guy called Jesse Mateman. The two of them got on well, and spent their time in Barcelona together. Sophie thought she'd met someone really special.

"My friend and I were on the rooftop having a drink. Jesse and his friends approached us and started chatting. I thought they were nice guys. We met up again a few days later, then spent the rest of our time with them. I slept with him in the hotel room and when I left and we returned to our respective countries (he was from Amsterdam), we spoke to each other every day.

"We'd talk about what we were up to, that we missed each other, and that we wanted to see each other again. He said he was going to visit me, but couldn't come over for a while, so I suggested visiting him."

He seemed really chuffed, so she packed her bags and spent £350 on a ticket to Amsterdam. She says Jesse was messaging her right up until she was getting on the plane, and was looking forward to her visit.

But when she arrived in Amsterdam, Jesse wasn't there to greet her as they had planned. Instead, she received a text saying, "You've been pigged." Sophie was devastated.

"Boys and their friends think it's funny but they don't think how scary it is for girls. It wasn't just being stood up, it was the shock and confusion. I panicked. I thought, 'If this guy is horrible and crazy enough to make me come all this way for a joke, what else is he capable of?'

"I was terrified he knew which hotel I was in, my name, my number. Was he planning on coming over, or stalking me? What if he turned up outside my hotel room?"

It's a horrible story, but I should add that Jesse denies

this version of events. He says he hardly knew Sophie, their contact was very short-lived, and the text messages did not come from him.

So, where does this all leave us? Too scared to date? Fearful that we are being ridiculed and mocked by anyone who shows us any interest? Of course not. It's unclear exactly how often 'pigging' is taking place – it takes a brave victim to stand up and admit to it – but I imagine it's very rare. What is vitally important is that we all call it out when it happens, or hear of it happening. That's why I have included the stories here.

Pigging is vile. The only pigs in both of the stories above were the men whose fragile egos led them to behave in such despicable ways. It goes without saying that not all men are like that. Of course, they aren't. The vast majority want the same from women as we want from men: a kind, warm and loving relationship.

What is also not widespread is the lunacy of the notion that thinness is essential for attractiveness. Men's tastes in women are as varied as women's tastes in men. Tastes depend on a variety of factors in a person's make up.

I visited Fiji many years ago (actually, come to think about it, not long after I'd finished with the 'pigging' boyfriend). When I arrived, I was comforted by locals, who brought fresh fruit to the hut I was staying in. They were desperately worried about my weight, and told me to eat up or I'd never find a man who wanted to marry me. For them, thinness was definitely not a sign of attractiveness. The gorgeous, curvy women with swinging hips, dressed in bright colours were to their tastes, not the slim woman from London who always dressed in black.

What is seen as attractive varies from continent to continent and through time.

Years ago, it was seen as inappropriate for women to be muscular. There's a lovely story about Joan Benoit who was the first woman to win a marathon at the Olympic Games. She won gold in 1984. Before that year, Olympic officials judged the marathon to be too difficult for women to do. When Benoit was training for the Games, she ran through the streets in the early morning before anyone was up. If a car drove past her, she pretended to be looking at the flowers, instead of running. "People would have thought it really odd to see a woman running through the streets back then," she said.

Doesn't that show how much we've changed. Today it would be odder to see a woman walking through the streets smelling flowers in the early morning than it would to see her running.

We have got used to seeing women as athletes and have become comfortable with the look and feel of a more toned and muscular body. As the 1980s progressed, aerobics classes became much more popular than they had before, and gyms began popping up everywhere. A healthy, toned body was what everyone was aiming for. This has endured. A study conducted by Frances Bozsik in 2019 suggests that 'thin and toned' is now the physique women are aspiring to achieve in the West.

So, be aware when wondering whether you have the 'ideal' body, that there's no such thing. When food is in short supply, rounded tummies are a sign of wealth and comfort and are admired. In times of plenty, skinniness is preferred. It's the same with everything – when most people worked out on the land and were nut brown in the summers, thanks to the sun's rays, being pale was seen as beautiful. Now everyone works in offices all day and rarely sees the sunlight, we consider a suntan as being a sign of wealth.

These tastes run in cycles through the generations. There are no absolutes, and personal taste varies a great deal from person to person.

So, how does all this relate to dating?

I think it's important to bear in mind that every country, every era and every person has a different idea of what 'attractiveness' looks like. It's important to remember that there aren't absolutes, and there's not a 'perfect figure'. Just be yourself and find someone who wants to be with you for more substantial reasons than what size you happen to be when you meet.

Dating tips

- Because it can be difficult to know when someone is being genuine when you first meet them (regardless of what size you are), the only answer is to take things as slowly as possible. Don't rush into any sort of intimacy until you are sure that the person is genuine.
- Be who you are. I know this is a terrible cliché, but it's true. You do not have to change yourself to be accepted by those who are worthy of you. If you feel yourself needing to change, or

thinking that you need to lose weight in order to keep him, he's not worth it.

- Remember, you don't have to be the one who is chosen, be the chooser. Stop worrying endlessly about whether you look right or whether anyone will fancy you, and start looking out there to see whether there are any men who you fancy.
- You are not a fat girl. You are a girl. Should you decide to lose weight let it be for yourself and not to get a boyfriend. When the right guy comes along, he will accept you as you are and appreciate you for what you are. Accept yourself.
- Whatever size you are, there is someone perfect for you...someone who will love you and cherish you and think you are the absolute perfect size. Because, when it comes to it, there are far more important things to consider when choosing a partner for life than whether they can fit into a pair of size 10 jeans!

ONLINE DATING

One of the novels in the Mary Brown series is called *Mary Brown is Leaving Town.* I wanted to write about online dating because it's difficult for women worried about their weight. When I researched the novel, one lady told me that she felt men could lie about their age and height in their profile pictures, and they would be forgiven for that when they arrived, just as women could do the same, but weight was non-negotiable. If you were bigger than the man expected you to be, he'd be gone in minutes.

This resonated with me, and I thought about it a lot as I wrote the novel: is weight really such a no-no? Does it matter to people so much more than other characteristics? It seems insane on many levels. You can lose weight, and over the course of a year, you could be a good few stone lighter or heavier than when you first meet someone.

Things like height and age are unchangeable, so they

would seem to be more important, but those I spoke to were insistent that weight was the one non-negotiable.

I have spoken to a mixture of people about their experiences of online dating when overweight, and all of them insisted that it was vitally important to introduce your weight into the conversation right from the start. The man needed to be very clear that you were big in order to avoid drama later on. Here are two points of view: a negative view of online dating and a much cheerier positive view.

The negative view

Stephanie Yeboah

Stephanie is a writer, fashion blogger and fat-acceptance advocate and has written extensively about her experiences of today's dating scene. This is her experience:

"As I paste my Instagram handle into the dating app conversation I've been having over the past three days, I make a private bet with myself to see how long it will take before the guy blocks or unmatches me after seeing my full-length photos. The record, as it currently stands, is four minutes.

"You see, dating as a fat person in today's society kinda sucks. Having only ever been in one relationship, and after being exposed to a roster of some of the most disgusting, dehumanising comments one could ever dream of while single, it's safe to say that my experience (or lack thereof) has been a bit of a shambles.

"I now send any potential matches the details of my

Instagram account (which features loads of full-length body shots, me without make-up and bikini shots) for them to peruse before taking the discussion any further. Le sigh.

"I am one of those women who adds the 'Fatter IRL' disclaimer to online profiles. I upload full-length, fabulous photos of myself in all my fat glory. I also tell my matches that I am indeed 'a fat'. Regardless, upon meeting them, I'm always met with the same pushbacks, from: 'You're not really my type physically,' to the fetishising 'I've never been with a big girl before,' 'I've heard fat girls are better at oral sex,' and the old favourite, 'More cushion for the pushin'!'

"Now I know how silly it is to have to declare our fatness; we shouldn't have to apologise for, and warn others of, our appearance because we are worthy and deserving of the same love, respect and basic human decency that others are entitled to.

"Society, unfortunately, still has an issue with those of us who do not fit into a size 16 or 18. As plus-size women, we are not afforded the same humanity, care, love and respect as our thinner counterparts. This can force a monumental drop in confidence and either put us off dating for life or lead us to more casual dating to try and prove our worth through sex.

"I believe that there is a special type of humiliation and trauma within dating that plus-size women can experience which completely ignores our personalities and instead focuses totally on our body shapes.

"What a lot of non-fat people don't know is that to

date while fat means you're put into three camps: being humiliated, being ignored or being fetishised.

"A great example of weight humiliation would be the utterly vile 'pull a pig' dating prank. In February I spoke about being the subject of such a prank on Bumble, in which I went on a couple of dates with a seemingly nice man and never heard from him again, only to later find out from a friend of his that they had bet him £300 to date a fat girl – a bet he evidently won.

"I initially felt humiliated, ashamed and completely dehumanised. I like to think that now I am confident enough and maybe numb enough to not let it define me as a woman, but for those of us who are still on our journey to finding self-love, going through an experience where you are basically seen as an experiment can be battering.

"As well as being humiliated, we also have to go through the daunting experience of being unmatched or blocked as soon as we send over a full-length photo of ourselves, or be resigned to being the fat best friend or the wing woman who gets to watch all their thinner friends be chatted up on nights out."

The positive view

Jennifer Abramovitz

"I'm a plus-size girl. I'm also a publicist, an extrovert, a bargain-shopper extraordinaire and an unbelievably good friend. But what's most visible about me, what defines me before I even open my mouth, is my size. I've dieted my whole life and can't remember a time when I wasn't concerned about my weight.

"I grew up with a mother who told me I was amazing, who said I could accomplish whatever I wanted to. She was supportive and loving. But when I was a teenager, she also started saying, 'You need to lose weight. It will be harder when you get older to find your partner.'

"I went to weight-loss camp when I was young and was introduced to boys and the bases. It was a different world there: Size wasn't so much of an issue, though there was a hierarchy, with the skinnier girls at the top. I had a few boyfriends every summer, and when I got really thin, I suddenly had a boyfriend back at school, too. That lasted for maybe a year. After that it was back to the old way, and I didn't have a boyfriend anymore.

"I didn't date at all in college. I was always overweight. Then my dad died when I was 22 and I wasn't interested in anything anymore. I was lost.

"It wasn't until I was 28 that I decided I wanted to date again, after I got back in touch with people from camp. Some of them were very heavy, but they were married and successful in relationships. I was like; why am I not dating?

"Friends of mine were setting one another up on dates but not me. It makes such an obvious statement—that no one would ever find me attractive because of my weight. I guess it's hard to say to somebody, 'I have a great girl for you, but she's fat—are you okay with that?' That makes me extremely uncomfortable and angry. People are image-conscious, and it takes a very secure man to advertise his preference for a woman of size.

"There's a misconception that plus-size girls are insecure in their bodies. Yes, there have been times I've felt uncomfortable at bars because guys talk to my friends and not me, and if I notice a group of men snickering at me, that always makes me upset. But my size has never stopped me.

"Then I started internet dating. It's not necessarily the viper's nest that people claim it is. When I started on BBW (Big Beautiful Women) dating sites, I got crazy amounts of e-mails. Before that, I didn't understand that there were people out there who preferred a round body with curves and boobs and a butt and lots of fat. Now I know that the skinny white girl is not the ideal to everyone. There are cultures and races that prefer plus-size women. I've had really in-shape guys, bodybuilders even, contact me. I think they like the juxtaposition of hard and soft. They like the feeling of being with someone who's bigger than they are and the voluptuousness of another body.

"A man approached me on the subway when I was 24 and wanted my phone number desperately. He kept saying over and over, 'I think you're beautiful.' My first instinct was, this is a joke, someone put him up to it—which says a lot about where I was at that point. It's not where I am now. Experience, age and understanding that a lot of people *are* attracted to me because of (or in spite of) my size takes away some of the nervousness I used to feel on dates.

"I've been seeing someone now who's given me a newfound perspective. He definitely cares about me and likes spending time with me, but if he could stare at my ass all day long, he would. He's opened my eyes to the fact that there are a lot of men out there who prefer plus-size women and that the pool isn't as small as I thought it was. And I feel very secure and confident when I'm with him."

Of course, you don't have to date (online or otherwise) at all. I'd like to finish this chapter with Lora Grady's refreshing attitude to her body and to the whole subject of dating

Lora Grady's story

"One morning after a fairly tense Thanksgiving dinner with my family, and I was sitting on my bed with my then-boyfriend Neal. He didn't know it yet, but we were about to break up. I'd known for days that this was something I needed to do. I had just spent two weeks in Europe, which helped me realized that I was done with his overbearing and sometimes creepy behaviour. (He once let himself into my best friend's house unannounced, when I wasn't even there, and just...sat down on her couch.) But even though I'd put a pillow in between us the night before, he was still caught off-guard when I told him we needed to go our separate ways. 'Can we take a break instead?' he asked. It had only been three months, so...no. Finally, after an awkward goodbye, it was done.

"At least I thought it was.

"That night, he started firing texts my way. His hurt had clearly turned to rage and it wasn't long before he started with the insults. 'You made my car bottom out!!!!' said one message. The lowered and souped-up-yet-shitty Honda Civic he treated better than me sat about an inch off the ground but sure, yes, it was my ass that caused it to scrape over speed bumps.

"Neal wasn't the first guy I dated who made critical comments about my weight, but he would be the last. His pathetic pleading followed by an actual tantrum finally made me realize that when he talked about my body, it was a sign of how insecure he was. It wasn't about me at all. And that made me realize that was probably true of my previous relationships, too.

"Like my first boyfriend, Zach. I was 16 and chatting on the phone with him while eating microwave popcorn when he said, 'Popcorn? That's junk food.' 'So?' I asked. I didn't like where this was going; I stopped eating. 'Yeah, you look good, so it doesn't really matter.' A sigh of relief. Then came the blow: 'But, you know, you could look a lot better.' I immediately teared up. At 16, I was intensely insecure about my body and a comment like that made me want to curl up into a ball and hide myself from the world.

"Fast forward to my second year of university. I was 19, living in downtown Toronto with roommates and totally in lust with Michael, a fitness trainer and model, whose jobs absolutely intimidated the hell out of me. We were snuggling on the couch and I was watching him eat pizza. (He didn't offer me any—massive red flag.) 'You're beautiful,' he told me. It was a nice moment—I felt comfortable, cute and relaxed. 'But you could be so much more beautiful if you lost some weight. Then, you'd be a 10.' He nodded to himself. Boom. Right in the heart. I tensed up and all over again, wanted to hide from him and the rest of the world that made me feel not good enough.

"All three of those asinine comments broke my heart a little bit. But that text from Neal about his car sent me over the edge. I'd officially had enough of the bullshit and was tired of feeling less than. Not long after I ditched him,

I discovered the body positive community on social media. I started seeing images and reading stories of women who unabashedly wore what they wanted and who were outspoken about being deserving. Slowly, I unlearned a lot of toxic tendencies.

"I used to think I had to settle for someone; that if I raised my standards too high, I'd end up alone forever. But facing my insecurities meant understanding that it is actually so much better to be on my own than to be with a partner who makes me feel worthless. My personhood and my self-esteem have to come first. I realized how lucky I was to ditch those dudes sooner rather than later.

"Now, at 31, I'm single and pretty damn happy. I've developed healthier boundaries and higher standards with guys and I've adopted a zero-tolerance policy when it comes to negative or unwanted comments about my body—from dates or anyone. I've also learned that there are, in fact, some men out there for whom I wouldn't have to settle to be with. But until one of them comes along, I'm happy to be in a committed, loving relationship with my own damn self."

HE'S PROPOSED: HELP, I NEED A WEDDING DRESS

I have to begin this chapter by telling you all about my friend. We'll call her Lucy. She's incredibly attractive. I really mean that. I know she's a friend and we all think our friends are fab, but she really is. She's got thick glossy hair and a beautiful face (she looks a lot like Holly Willoughby). Added to that, she's bright, interesting and great fun. She's about a size 18 (UK), and she carries it so well that her weight is the last thing you notice about her. Until the day we went to find her a wedding dress.

Oh my God. We were made to feel very well aware of her weight then.

When Lucy said she was after a wedding dress, the assistants in the first shop looked at us pityingly, and stared at Lucy as if she had three arms. Lucy started talking through the sort of dress she wanted and how she wanted it to look from the back and what sort of neckline she was after. The woman was clearly thinking: "She's fat. I will bring her the fat dresses."

We knew it would be hard, of course. But we were still surprised by how hard it was. Lucy is only one size above the UK average size – she's closer to the average size than the size 10 girls who were swanning around the shop with hundreds of styles to choose from.

The rest of our day didn't pan out much better.

We went to eight shops in all, and it felt as if each was less welcoming as we proceeded. By the end, we were all flabbergasted. The assistants had squeezed my lovely friend into any dresses they had in her size, then draped her in veils and tiaras even though it was very clear she wanted neither. While they fussed over the slimmer girls and stood them on blocks so the dress fell beautifully and looked amazing, they left Lucy standing there in shoes which didn't fit, and seemed keen, all the time, to move on and help someone else. We left each one at speed and eventually went and got wine.

We made light of the whole thing, and Lucy went on to get a dress hand-made with a corset fitted into it (top tip – a corset in a wedding dress makes everything look much better) but we learned a few things along the way. Here they are:

- There's nothing quite like standing around in your underwear in front of a complete stranger (or even your mother for that matter) while being squeezed into dresses meant for the 'average' size woman when you ARE the average-size woman.

- Repeatedly being told that: "Nothing's going to fit you in here, honey," is quite frustrating. Once again: at size 18, you are close to the average size of a woman, so it's tempting to ask the assistant, "Why is nothing going to fit me, honey?"
- The assistants will comment on how 'much smaller' you look in certain dresses, as if the only thing that matters is which dress will make you look thin. There are other parameters: like whether the colouring suits me, whether it makes me happy, can I move in it, can I dance in it? Will it fill me with joy?
- "We have two dresses in your size. I'll bring them and you can choose which one you want." This is what my friend was told in one shop. She said: "If you only have two dresses here, I doubt I'll like either." I take her point. Most 'normal weight' brides can try on dozens of dresses, yet my friend was treated as though she ought to be very grateful to have one to try on.
- You will hear all sorts of words to describe your figure. From 'curvy' to 'larger lady', 'big girl', 'solid build', and 'voluptuous' to 'childbearing figure'. My friend is 53. I'm not sure that child bearing is on top of her list of things to do.
- There will be an assumption that you are planning to lose weight for the wedding. Assistants in wedding shops will ask: "So, are we planning on losing any weight for the big day?"

- Incase you're wondering, my friend married her lovely boyfriend on a sunny day last summer and they are living happily ever after. She's still a size 18 and still gorgeous.

SECTION SIX

HOLIDAYS AND CHRISTMAS

HOLIDAYS

You've decided to go off on holiday – the lure of the open road, the freedom from responsibilities and commitments, just you and a world to explore. Whether it's five days in Magaluf or a 10-week cruise around the Caribbean, travelling is wonderful.

But it can be difficult. Once you've found your passport and ticket and thrown them into your rucksack with your phone and your swimming costume, you jump on the bus and make your way to the airport. The bus winds its way along, heading towards Heathrow. You spot a plane in the sky; you're getting closer, your heart gives a little jump of excitement. You'll soon be at the airport. This is going to be fantastic. FANTASTIC.

At this point, if you're slim, you'll start to think about yourself on the plane, gliding between the clouds while you sip a gin and tonic, whiling away the hours until you touch down and dive into the silky blue waters of some foreign ocean.

If you're fat, it's not that straightforward: you're thinking...shit, will the seat belt go round me? If it doesn't, who should I ask for an extension? What if they don't have extension belts...will they let me fly? Shit, what if they don't? And what if the seats are really small and I'm bulging out of them? I bet no one will want to sit next to me. And so it goes on.

The joys of travelling to new and unexpected places can be tarnished by fears about what to expect from the journey and what you will encounter when you get there. So here is your 12-point guide to travelling as a fat person.

1. Am I too fat to fly?

The short answer to this is 'no'. People of all shapes and sizes travel around the world every day. I tend to get onto the plane, and as soon as I see the air hostess, I indicate my figure by running my hands down myself and shrugging apologetically. In many years of travelling as an overweight person, this has never failed to get a knowing nod and the arrival of a seat-belt extender. If you're lucky, she'll bring it over surreptitiously, and hand it to you like you're involved in some sort of secret drug deal. If you're unlucky she'll scream, "Fatty in seat 12A needs a seat-belt extender." For the record, I have never encountered someone behaving like that latter example!

If you're really worried about the whole seat-belt extender situation, you can buy your own for about a tenner and take it with you.

One other reassurance to make is that they won't

weigh you. A friend almost cancelled her holiday to Canada because she heard a rumour that people would be weighed before getting on the plane. You're not luggage. They won't weigh you.

2. Which seat can I have?

There shouldn't be any problem with the seating when you get on the plane, but if you are very large and thus do not fit into an economy seat, some airlines will insist that you buy a second seat. So, if you are concerned that this might apply to you, it is always worth checking in advance to avoid any problems or delays on the day of your flight. One other thing to mention is that if you are overweight, this might prevent you from sitting in exit rows. Again, if you want to avoid any awkwardness, it might be worth checking your ticket number (sites like https://www.seatguru.com will show you exactly where your seat is). If you have an exit seat, you may like to talk to airline officials before boarding.

3. Security

I know that airport security scanners can be an issue for some people. Not because you are trying to carry guns or knives through, but because if your body touches the sides of the machine, it beeps. Not ideal. So, if you're worried about this happening, it's worth explaining your fears to someone. Better that than going through it, having it bleep and finding yourself mortified with embarrassment.

. . .

4. Rickshaws and tuk-tuks etc

A friend visited Bangkok recently and thought it would be fun to ride in a tuk-tuk, so she and her sister headed towards one and stated their destination. "No, no," he said. "Whole thing tip over. Not good." Just to make sure she completely understood what he was staying, he leaned over while he was speaking, mimicking the bang onto the floor and filling his cheeks with air to make it absolutely clear that this was because she was fat. Nice. It's worth checking what the situation is wherever you're going. The rickshaws vary a lot in strength and size.

5. Buses

Just a quick warning: bus turnstiles in some countries are very narrow to squeeze through. A newspaper report from 1994 describes a 'large western woman' getting stuck in the turnstiles and having to be cut out. Now I'm sure there are more embarrassing things that could happen on a bus, but it's hard to think of too many. Forewarned is forearmed.

6. Fascination

Anyone who has been pregnant knows how touchy-feely people get with you; they want to touch your stomach because they are genuinely fascinated. In many countries, especially those where there aren't many overweight people, the general population will show the same fascination for fat people.

I went to India a few years ago, and was surrounded wherever I went by young children staring at me, and wanting to touch me. As I walked through the streets I felt like the Pied Piper, with a stream of children running behind me. Whenever I turned around and smiled at them, they would run away, shrieking with laughter. Eventually I found out what was going on, and – I have to say – it wasn't wildly flattering.

"Hey, lady. Are you Buddha?" one of the children shouted. They all crowded around me and stared at me. "Big Buddha stomach."

Yes, OK, thanks very much, I get it.

7. What will people say when they see me in a bikini?

This is the thing that many overweight people hate more than anything else. The truth is that it doesn't matter what other people think or say. If they have a problem then THEY have a problem. Not you. You just lie there in all your curvy fabulousness and enjoy the sunshine. You're not the one with the problem; they are.

8. Cultural ideals

At the beginning of the book I mentioned going to Fiji in my 20s and being stared at in the streets for being so skinny. I was a size 10 and the men said I would never make strong babies so no man would want me. At the same weight you could go into a designer dress shop in

Paris and be told that you are too big to fit into any of the clothes. Every country has a different body image ideal. So, in some countries, your voluptuous curves will be seen as attractive. In others, they'll get you scowls. That's why you can't take it all too seriously. Just be as healthy as you can, be kind to yourself, and sod everyone else.

9. Towels

There's every chance that the towel you will get in the hotel will be roughly the same size as a face cloth, so if you want a towel that will go safely around you without exposing your private parts to all and sundry, I suggest you take your own. I know it's a pain to pack a towel, but – honestly – you'll regret it if you don't.

10. Avoid top bunks

This isn't even just a fat girl thing; top bunks are terrifying. As are bottom bunks. As a general rule: avoid bunk beds altogether.

11. Shoes

Get yourself some decent shoes that support your feet, don't give you blisters and won't fall apart on the first day. Remember that your feet will swell in the heat, so don't buy shoes that are too tight-fitting.

12. Give yourself a break

One final point I'd like to make is that if you're going off travelling or on holiday, you are going to enjoy a change from the norm, so give yourself a break from trying to look good; relax and have fun. Everyone knows that as soon as it's over 80 degrees, you can't look good. No one can. It's not going to happen.

Instead, concentrate on swimming in the sea at night, walking in the moonlight, dancing in foreign bars and having yourself a brilliant time without worrying for one second about being judged or whether people approve of you. Just relax and allow yourself to enjoy life.

CHRISTMAS

No handbook which looks at life as an overweight person would be complete without a small chapter about Christmas – the most amazing time of year when all anyone wants to do, from morn til night, is eat, drink and complain about eating and drinking too much.

On any given Christmas Day, research shows that the average woman is putting things into her mouth every three seconds. (That's made-up research, but you know what I mean. THERE IS NO END TO THE EATING.) The food doesn't even have to make sense. You want a mashed potato and peanut butter sandwich with pickled onions and chocolate sauce? That's fine. Go ahead. It's Christmas. You can eat whatever you like. And drink whatever you like. If you want half a pint of Baileys before breakfast, you're not being a crazy alcoholic, you're being a good sport at Christmas. I really don't remember a Christmas when I didn't eat half a box of chocolates before breakfast. It's bonkers.

And that's before we get onto all the huge meals featuring a choice of meats, every vegetable known to man and roughly 58 tons of roast potatoes. It's wonderful, and we should all be grateful that we can afford to eat so lavishly and have families to spend time with, but it is very confusing if you're prone to overeating. I know many of us don't know how to stop eating on a normal day, but when people are delighting in food so overtly, it can be particularly difficult.

The overindulgence is followed by disappointment and overcompensation in terms of not eating anything but grass for the whole of Boxing Day. Until the evening when you give up and eat all the left-overs and every chocolate in the house, including the kids'.

Still, you tell yourself, it's OK because this year's nearly over and next year will definitely be the one in which I sort myself out and lose all the weight. My New Year's Resolution will be to lose weight and start feeling good about myself. I should say that I make this resolution even as I'm tipping chocolates and pastry snacks down my throat at considerable speed.

The result of all this eating wildly before regretting it and trying to make amends with myself is like some sort of food-inspired self-flagellation.

I have a friend with an eating disorder who has come to loathe Christmas because of what it does to her mental health. Bingeing at Christmas is fun if you're able to go back to a normal way of eating afterwards, but if it throws you into a cycle of self-hatred then, obviously, it's not so good. A gossamer-thin layer of guilt sits over the whole occasion.

"You have to reach out and talk about it if you can," says Dr Eileen Atkinson.

"There can be sympathy in solidarity. It's useful to talk about how you're feeling before you start to feel so low that you binge eat solidly for three days, or eat nothing, because you feel so bad.

"Hopefully you'll find confidence in shared experiences. Whatever you do – don't lock yourself away and refuse to go out in the misguided view that this will make you feel better about everything. That's not the answer."

Dr Atkinson is right that many people lock themselves away and don't go to parties and social occasions at Christmas because they are not feeling good. A survey from vouchercloud.com asked 2,000 women why they might skip a social occasion. The top reason women gave? Yes, you've guessed it: 'I was having a fat day.' This was given by over half the respondents for a reason they might miss a party. Below this came:

- I couldn't find an outfit to wear
- I didn't have enough time to get ready
- I wanted to stay home and watch TV
- I was having troubles with my relationship

This means that most women, when they decide to miss parties at Christmas, do so because of their fears about the way they look. It's a bit depressing really.

So, the final message about Christmas is this – relax and do what makes you happy. If you don't want to go to endless Christmas parties and want to stay in and watch repeats of *Morse*, that's fine. But if there's a party you want to go to, please go, enjoy yourself and try not to worry about what people are thinking.

Your friends want to see you because they like you. They would be heartbroken if they thought you had missed a fun night out because you were worried they might think you were fat. Those who love you don't care; those who don't love you aren't worth worrying about.

Enjoy Christmas, try not to worry endlessly about overeating – it's just one day in the year, and go to those parties. Life is WAY too short to miss out on parties.

SECTION SEVEN

EXERCISING

WHAT IS EXERCISE?

I have a very complicated relationship with exercise, as I'm sure you do, too. On the one hand, I can watch people running, listening to music as they fly down the street or across fields, and I think how wonderful it looks to be lost in your own thoughts, escaping from the world, enjoying the freedom of time by yourself. How lovely, and uplifting.

I'm the same when I see people doing dance classes or Zumba classes on television or in YouTube clips. As they shake their booties to the lively beats, I feel a warm glow thinking how good it would feel to be in the class with friends, all lost in the music and enjoying the moment.

But – and this is where the complicated relationship bit comes in – the reality of actually putting on my gym kit, going to the gym and sweating like a giant pig in Lycra while having to look at myself in the mirror, shaking and dancing around, is really the definition of hell on earth. Just 10 minutes in a Zumba class and I'm ready to give up on life entirely.

It's the same with the lovely runs through the countryside. Yeah, it looks great when you see women with long hair, with daisy chains round their pretty little necks, cycling through country lanes in summer dresses and sandals. But the truth is that it's winter and I live in the city. I don't pass all that many daisy-strewn country lanes – just mad couriers who weave in and out, practically knocking you into the traffic, and buses that change lanes without offering a moment's notice.

Running is about freezing half to death in the early winter mornings, and feeling awful for the rest of the day. And it's not just the morning that is ruined by the run… There is the night before as well.

It's easy to think of the romance of an early morning run when you're not actually planning to do one. But if you are genuinely going to get up at 5 am, the night before is spent in a state of anger at the fact that you've got to get up so early, and frustration that you have to go to bed early. Then, when the alarm rings out its torturous tune at 5 am, naturally, you lean over and switch it off, opting for another hour of sleep instead of hitting the streets.

Later in the day I'll see a picture of a glamorous blonde running along a white sand beach and think, "Ah, I should have done that this morning. I'm definitely doing it tomorrow…" and the whole cycle begins again.

It's just so hard to be motivated to do any exercise, even though we all know it will make us feel better, make our skin glow and make us feel psychologically more engaged with the world.

I've tried to work out why I find it so hard to make

myself actually do anything rather than just think about it, and I suspect it's because I had a little bit of trauma in the exercise department, which I should probably tell you about.

After leaving university, I took a part-time job in a gym while writing my first book. I thought it was a job on reception, and was quite able to take people's money, scan in their membership card, and give them locker keys if they'd forgotten theirs, as well as book them in to step aerobics or whatever particular class it was that they wanted to go to. It didn't seem any more complicated than working in a supermarket.

So, I turned up on my first day, and it was all fine. Lots of gorgeous 20-year-olds in size 8 bubble-gum pink Lycra came streaming past me and into the gym or classes and it was fine. I sat there, scanned their cards and made polite conversation. I made some changes to make things easier for everyone by laying out the list of classes so that people could see exactly what was on as soon as they walked in. It made the whole thing function much better.

"That's brilliant," said John, the guy who owned the gym. "I don't know why we didn't think of doing that – it's much easier if people can just tick off the class they want to go to."

I thanked him, and felt a rush of pleasure that my time there wasn't entirely wasted.

"And you take your first class this afternoon, don't you?" he added. I hadn't said anything about wanting to do any classes, so I just half smiled at him.

At 2.50 that afternoon he came over, and said, "Off

you go then. I'll man the reception while you're in the class."

"OK," I said reticently. I didn't have any desire to do a step aerobics class, but I was young and fit, so I was happy to do it if he really wanted me to. Especially if it was a way of keeping the job. I supposed, if I was honest with myself, it would be better to have done some of the classes so that when people asked about them, I could answer honestly and with some experience.

But that's when it all started to go wrong.

I walked into the aerobics class, and saw about 25 people standing there staring at the front. I joined them, standing at the back of the room, and they all turned round to face me.

"Are you doing it this way?" asked one of the women.

"Sorry?" I said.

"The instructor usually stands that side – at the front of the room."

"I'm not the instructor," I said.

"Yes, you are," said David, walking into the room and handing me a microphone pack.

"Have fun."

Now at this stage, I think that every sane person would have said: "There's been a mistake, I'm not an aerobics tutor, I can't do this."

But I was quite enjoying the job, and I was young and fit, so why not give it a go? Besides, it's hard to refuse to do something that the boss has asked you to do, when you're young. For some reason I thought I might be able to wing it. I couldn't.

After a certain amount of fiddling with the music

system, and some help from the ladies at the front of the class, I got the music going...booming out into the room. I told the women to step from side to side as I had seen classes do in the past.

"To the left," I said. "And to the right." Unfortunately, I left them stepping side to side for about 10 minutes because I didn't know what else to do, then I asked them to skip around the room. They skipped around the room for about 10 minutes, then I assembled them back in the middle and did more stepping from side to side, this time with shaking arms in the air. Then I shouted, "Freestyle!" and leapt around like a loony, assuming they would join in with me. When I looked out at them, they were just looking back at me in absolute horror. Half of them had gone, and minutes later, while I was still freaking out in my 'freestyle' way, David came into the room and switched the music off.

"Ladies, we'll leave the class there for today, but your normal tutor will be back next week. Thank you very much, Bernice."

They didn't sack me from the job, but I was too embarrassed to go back there, and got my mum to phone up and say I wasn't very well and would have to leave. I saw David a few weeks later in Marks and Spencer. I dived behind the breaded chicken, hoping he wouldn't spot me. He did of course, and then thought I was even more insane for throwing myself behind the poultry section.

I hope your experiences of exercise are more positive, and less humiliating!

. . .

BEFORE WE START LOOKING at exercise in any depth, I want to share a universal truth with you: when you walk into the gym or an exercise class or just start speed walking round the park, it will feel like everyone but you is glowing with health and vitality as they exercise; managing to look serene and beautiful as they train. You will watch them as they leap with the grace of a gymnast, notice their glossy hair flying behind them and not a trace of actual real sweat, and you will scowl and probably want to hit them very hard with a brick.

But no. Move away from the brick. The thing to remember is that everyone – I mean EVERYONE – thinks that they look awful in the gym and thinks that everyone else looks good. I've never come across anyone who thinks they look good in sweat-stained gym wear. So, give yourself a break. However bad you feel – so does everyone else. And they are far too preoccupied with the way they look to give you a second glance.

So – please – don't be put off by worrying about how you look. It's only by doing exercise, and feeling the health and fitness benefits of it, that you'll start to realise how vitally important it is. If you find exercises that you enjoy, in which you'll make new friends and feel happy and flooded with endorphins, it doesn't matter what you look like and whether you're eight stone or 28 stone.

The other thing about exercise is that it's important whether you want to lose weight or not. Even if you are completely comfortable in the way you look, it's important to exercise for health as well as fitness reasons.

If you do want to lose weight, I think it's crucial to incorporate exercise into your routine. And it's not because of calories lost while exercising. The truth is, it can be depressing to spend 10 minutes on a cross trainer and realise you've only used up 20 calories. No, it's much deeper than that. We all know that weight loss demands a mental shift, and exercising can help with that. Just to repeat:

It's my view that exercise helps you make the crucial mental shift required to lose weight.

It does this in five key ways:

1. It makes you aware of consequences

Once you start training and putting work in at the gym, you will be less likely to reach for Mars bars and takeaways. You'll think of all the effort it took to run on the treadmill for 10 minutes and not want to ruin it all. If you don't exercise it's much easier to reach for takeaways without thinking of the consequences.

2. It gives you measure of achievement

The gym gives you a measure of achievement that can be alluring. You turn up and walk for five minutes, then build to 10 minutes, then set yourself a goal of 15 minutes, and soon you are lifting weights/running/cycling/attending classes that you never would have thought possible a few weeks previously. You can measure the difference and really see the numbers go up, which can keep you coming back and give you something positive to focus on.

. . .

3. It puts you into a healthy environment

Research shows us that many people put on weight because they are around other people who eat and drink a lot and they become socialised into that way of behaviour. It becomes 'normal' to have a takeaway every night, or drink every night.

Research published in the 'New England Journal of Medicine' concluded that people were most likely to become obese when a friend or others in their peer group were obese. "That factor alone increased an individual's chances of becoming obese by 57%." So, you don't have to dump all your friends, but if you have found yourself in an environment in which everyone eats and drinks too much, step out of it and into a healthier environment a few times a week, and see what a difference it makes.

In the gym/at Park Run/at the local sports centre or just running through the park, you will be around people who care about their bodies, want to look fit and are healthier, by and large, than those in McDonald's and the pub. It should make a crucial difference to your mindset and habits around food.

4. It gets the endorphins flowing

As we'll learn in the section on people who have lost weight, many people put on weight because they felt negative about life, and a bit hopeless. Feeling brighter, more energised and happier is an important part of fighting the mental battle. Exercise will literally get the endorphins flowing and make you feel happier, which in turn puts you in a better frame of mind for weight loss.

. . .

5. You see the difference in yourself

One of the hardest things about losing weight is that it takes so long to make a difference. Most people give up within a few weeks because the effort they are putting in isn't matched by the results they are achieving. Going to the gym is good to do alongside any weight-loss programme because you start to get results much quicker. You can really see and feel the difference in yourself. Within a few weeks you'll notice that you can run for the bus more easily, you'll feel the muscles aching from where you've used them. You will feel the difference in yourself. This is hugely motivating.

So, in conclusion: fitness is good. Now, in the next section we will take a look at what fitness is, then there's an A–Z of exercises available, and how you can cope with them if you're a few stone over fighting weight but fancy having a go. Just don't expect instant fitness – stick at it. And don't be afraid to give something new a go. Don't let your weight or size hold you back from achieving what you want to. The more you do it, the easier it gets and the more you will enjoy it.

WHAT IS FITNESS?

This sounds like a straightforward question – but it's a bit more complicated than it first appears – fitness and health are not the same things. To be healthy requires lots of things like nutrition and fresh air, fitness is just one component of health. The other thing is that health is a general term – it means having the right components in place to live the best life you can, free of illness and injury.

Fitness is slightly different – you get fit for something, rather than aim for a general ideal. And the thing you want to get fit for is what will determine the exercise that you do: fitness for rugby is different to fitness for gymnastics, but if you want to be fit for health reasons, you need a balance of the different components of fitness.

But, I hear you cry, what are the components of fitness? The truth is that there are loads, and we could look at: agility, balance, coordination, power, reaction time, body composition, muscle endurance, muscle strength and speed. But we're not training for the bloody

Olympics, we're just trying to keep ourselves a little bit healthier. So, in the spirit of that, we will break fitness down into three basic elements that spell the word: ASS (aerobic, suppleness and strength).

Aerobic fitness

This is, basically, any exercise in which you find yourself getting out of breath and having to take in oxygen. So, things like:

- Walking
- Dancing
- Swimming
- Water aerobics
- Jogging and running
- Aerobic exercise classes
- Cycling
- Some gardening activities, such as raking and pushing a lawn mower
- Tennis
- Golf

Suppleness training

Any exercise in which you are gently stretching the muscles. This will help with injury prevention and is particularly useful for keeping up mobility as you get older.

- Stretching
- Yoga
- Tai Chi
- Body balance
- Pilates

Strength

In a nutshell, this involves activities that work your muscles.

It is important to remember not to lift weights that are too heavy and likely to cause injury, and it's important to work muscles all over your body and not just your arms and chest (we've all seen the pictures of guys with skinny legs and bulging biceps). If you want to include weight training in your fitness routine and don't know what you're doing, it's ALWAYS best to ask someone at the gym.

THE A–Z OF FITNESS ACTIVITIES

Right, so now it's time to get going on the list of activities that you could consider doing. In the interests of providing as much information as possible, here is an A–Z of various types of exercise that will keep you fit, allow you to meet people and will give you a figure like Kate Moss* (unable to guarantee this last one).

Aerobics

Remember when aerobics first started? My recollections are of seeing Jane Fonda 'feel the burn' in Lycra and ankle warmers. Loud music, bright colours and lots of moving around. The pace was relentless and the impact was great. Most of the people teaching those classes in the early 1980s are now struggling with dodgy hips and aching ankles. We've learned a lot since those early, heady days.

The truth is that you don't have to go mental to enjoy aerobics classes. Most gyms and sports centres these days have a range of classes to suit all needs and abilities. It's inspiring to exercise to music, and uplifting to join in with a group of people. Well worth trying out legs, bums and tums, Zumba, wake-up workout and all the other variants to find one you like. The great thing about them is that they usually have 'high' and 'low' options, so the instructor will do the routine and you follow as best you can, cutting out the jumps and bounces if you don't feel up to them. No one will judge. Just work at your own pace.

Boxercise

The development of sports into gym classes occurred because of people's desire to look like sportsmen and women. Classes exist in cycling, rowing, boxing, gymnastics, dance, belly dancing and many other disciplines in which the key components of the sports training are taken and put into a class. The result is a series of fun classes, set to music, in which you get to pretend you're Rocky or Bradley Wiggins.

Boxercise is really good fun. It's hard work, but the fact that you're concentrating on whether you're jabbing, upper cutting or throwing left hooks distracts you from realising that you're moving non-stop. Well worth trying. Much more fun than you think it's going to be. You don't have to know anything about boxing and no one is going to punch you really hard.

Cycling

One of the great attractions of cycling regularly is that it's useful as well as being a great way to keep fit. If you can cycle to and from work, or even cycle to meet friends or go to the shops, it allows you to combine your exercise with a journey. And it's outside. The downsides are that it's not so much fun when it's cold, and depending where you live, you might have to cycle on main roads and fight with the traffic. But if there is a park nearby that you can cycle to, and if it is a nice day, it's the perfect way to take in some exercise (but buy those padded shorts or you'll start to feel hugely uncomfortable in unmentionable places if you cycle for any distance without them).

Dance

This is one of the loveliest ways to exercise. There are all sorts of dance classes available in gyms and studios – from ballet classes to 'barre' classes, 'Silver Swan' classes (ballet for older ladies – worth googling), to the Zumba and upbeat dance classes mentioned earlier.

Strictly has led to a rise in ballroom dancing classes, so even if you're not very mobile but want to get moving, you can get involved by signing up for classes in village halls and salsa dancing studios. Gyms, pubs and theatres have dancing classes and you rarely need to be a member to join in. Get on Google and have a look at what's available in your area.

Exergaming

This is where you use a games console to exercise, so

you can exercise in the comfort of your own home but while being pushed on by a machine in the corner of the room. You can do dancing classes, yoga, Pilates and all types of fitness classes on Wii, PlayStation and Xbox. It's worth taking a look at what's available. Obviously, there are also lots of free classes online and available on your mobile as an app as well. It can be a good way to start exercising if you want to follow someone and be told what to do next, but don't feel ready to join a class.

Football

Did you see the 2019 FIFA Women's World Cup? The women looked fit, strong and beautiful. As a result of England's success in the tournament, and the massive amount of media coverage it generated, there are more women and girls playing football than ever before. There are lots of 'come and try it' days for women of all ages. You can even do walking football if the game at full throttle feels like it might be too much. Your local council is a good place to start looking for classes, or you could drop a line to the Football Association and see whether they can help you to locate a local club. Remember, no one's expecting you to play like Lionel Messi – it's just a chance to run around with a group of like-minded women, get fit and have fun!

Gym

Walking into a gym and not knowing what to do, or doing something wrong, was one of my biggest concerns when I first went back to exercising. I thought everyone was watching me as I walked across to the apparatus without any idea what to do. But, do you know what I learned pretty quickly? At the risk of repeating myself: nobody is looking at you. Honestly, you're lovely and well worth looking at, but no one is actually looking at you! Serious gym goers are far too busy breaking a sweat and surviving their workouts to care who else is in the gym, and posers are too busy staring at their reflections. Fellow newcomers will be wandering around looking a little bit lost. So, don't worry.

The other thing to remember is that the gym is not as scary a place as it might seem. You can go for a gentle walk on the treadmill or a leisurely ride on a stationary bike while watching television or listening to music – you don't have to go all Arnold Schwarzenegger. There are always gym staff around to help and advise you, and loads of different machines and equipment to try. Once you get used to it, you'll find it all fairly straightforward and, sometimes, enjoyable.

Just remember to buy a sports bra.

Hockey

Much the same as with the football – when Team GB won hockey gold in the 2016 Olympic Games, there was a surge of interest in the sport, lots of clubs were opened and women were encouraged to take up sticks for the first time since school. Getting involved in a sport is a great way to exercise because your focus shifts from the exercise to the game and you find yourself exercising by default. You really don't have to be aiming for a place in the next Olympics to go along. Lots of the people there will be like you; keen to try the sport and get fit. Again, the local council can advise you where to go for classes, courses and leagues, or www.EnglandHockey.co.uk has a 'find a club' section through which you can put in your postcode and find the nearest place to play. Indeed, if you're anywhere in the UK, not just England, their system works. I've just tried it with lots of postcodes outside England and it comes up with local clubs across the country.

Just one thing – if you end up making it into the GB squad, and win Sports Personality of the Year, remember to mention me in your speech and how this book kick-started your international career.

Indoor activity

I have decided to do a separate 'exercising at home' section for everyone who wants to take up exercising but doesn't want to be in public just yet. This is in Chapter Twenty at the end of this section.

Jogging

I've called this jogging, rather than running, because as soon as I saw running written on the page, I thought it sounded like an Olympic sport, and no one is expecting you to buy spikes and break Usain Bolt's world record. But some fast walking, speeding into gentle jogging, in which you swing your arms a little and build up some speed so your heart rate is higher – well that's all you need to do. If it gets too much, stop and go back to walking.

If you challenge yourself to insert a longer jog into your walk every time you go out, you'll find yourself building up quite quickly. Try that thing where you run between one set of lamp posts, then walk between the next set. This process of alternating walking and running is called Fartlek training, and it's a great way to begin because your heart rate never slows right down, so you keep on burning those pesky calories and improving your stamina.

If you don't want to go out running by yourself, there are loads of running groups around. Look out for Park Run – truly the greatest gift of all to the fledgling jogger. I have three friends who joined Park Run and went every week, walking at first, then building up so they now run 5 km every Saturday. They all look much better and have made lots of friends. One of them has lost a colossal six stones along the way.

Take a look on https://www.parkrun.org.uk/ for more information. Just make sure you get yourself some decent training shoes before you set off. Chuck out those old plimsoles that you wore in junior school and invest in shoes that will cushion your feet and help to prevent ankle, knee, hip and back injuries.

Kettlebell

No – not a little bell that you ring when you want a cup of tea, though heaven knows that would be nice!

These are those unlikely looking things you might have seen lying around if you go to the gym. They look like military grade weapons…the sort of thing you might find left lying around on a battlefield.

Now, I know I'm not making them sound like a great deal of fun, but the thing is – they work. And when I say 'work', I mean they target all areas of your body from core to legs, to arms and abs. All you have to do is swing them. You need to get the swing right, so you'll need to get someone in the gym to show you so you don't hurt yourself, but once you get the hang of it, they're very good.

Swing them down between your legs and up to your shoulder and you'll have found yourself a nifty little all-body toning machine that's the size of a football.

But as I said earlier – please do make sure you get proper specialist instruction before you start wildly swinging them round. And if you're not a member of a gym but like the sound of them, most sports centres have gyms that you can access for around £5, so it would be worth going along, and talking to the instructors there about them.

Lawn bowls

Quite a different vibe to kettlebells. It's not the most dramatic sort of exercise, but it is exercise and you will be outside and you'll be playing with other people. If you can convince yourself to walk there and walk back as well, it's all much more active than watching *Killing Eve* with a pizza. There are lots of leagues and clubs in most parks, and it will get your competitive juices flowing while giving you fresh air and exercise.

Martial arts

Whether it's ju-jitsu or t'ai chi – there's a lot more to martial arts than smashing bits of wood in two with your head, and Jackie Chan films. They are organised, disciplined sports which require a great deal of strength and flexibility. You'll work out your whole body and feel empowered and confident in the process. It's worth taking a look at the various different disciplines on offer…they vary enormously. Many of them have women-only classes and over-50s classes in case you're worried about being the only woman in the group, or surrounded by teenagers!

Netball

Your memories of playing this sport at school are bound to entirely colour your view of it as an adult. Was it a fun way to pass the time – running around in the sunshine with your friends? Or, perhaps it brings back memories of ugly PE knickers and mottled legs as you shivered in the rain? But – please – if your memories are of the latter scenario, don't write the sport off completely. Netball is on the up at the moment, and has achieved a bigger profile than ever before thanks to the surge in coverage of women's sports, and big successes at international level. There are clubs and leagues all over the country and lots of beginners' classes.

. . .

Orienteering (walking)

There is no question that walking is one of the best ways of retaining a level of fitness, keeping joints mobile, and raising your heart rate. A brisk walk every day will make a huge difference to your fitness, it's also a great way to see places, and lots of clubs do walks through lovely parks, across hills, mountains, fields and valleys, giving you the opportunity to combine fitness training with sightseeing. It's worth incorporating a walk into your day, whether it's getting off the bus a stop earlier, or going the whole hog and joining an orienteering club.

Personal training

Personal training is a great way to get into fitness, and keep developing your fitness so you're working as hard as you can every time you go to the gym or park. Obviously, the thing holding many people back from hiring a personal fitness trainer is the cost, but if you want to invest a little bit in your fitness this is a really good idea, especially if you team up with a friend or two and split the cost. Also, it's worth talking to personal trainers in the gym, because they often do a free session with you and give you a programme that you can follow, and follow-up sessions with them when you finish it.

It's very motivating, and it's amazing how much harder you work, and just how much further you can push yourself, when there is someone else watching and instructing. It goes without saying, of course, that you need a reliable, trustworthy and professional personal trainer to ensure you don't do yourself more damage than good!

Quick sessions

The HIIT exercise revolution (high intensity interval training) has been an absolute game changer for people who don't have much time, but are very keen to get as fit as possible in the time they have. What it involves is working really hard for a short period of time so that you scorch the muscles and leave them working long after you finish your session. If you can fit in blasts for 15 minutes every other day, you'll make a real difference to your fitness, especially if you combine this with trying to walk as much as possible during the day. It's worth having a look for 'HIIT' sessions on the internet. There's lots of information on there, details about where classes are held, and sessions you can do online.

Rope

I've called this 'rope' rather than skipping, because I think of skipping as an activity that we did at junior school, singing songs while we jumped in and out. Rope training is skipping with attitude! It's what boxers and dancers do to get that lean, mean shape. You can pick up a skipping rope from a sports shop or from Amazon for less than a tenner and skip to your heart's content. If you go onto Google and put in 'skipping rope workouts' you'll get lots of videos showing you 10-minute beginner sessions as well as more advanced training. It's well worth giving it a go.

Swimming

It's non-weight-bearing, so if you're overweight and worried that doing exercise will put undue pressure on your limbs, this might be the one to go for. It's relaxing, allows you to switch off, and uses your whole body. There are classes for improving your swimming, which will encourage you to try ways of going faster, and developing your stroke. They are great ways of getting fit, and you can feel yourself developing as you do more lengths. If you haven't swum for a while, there are lots of beginners' groups where you can go to regain your confidence.

Tennis

This is such a great, sociable sport: one which gives you fresh air, fitness and the chance to talk to like-minded individuals. You can play at all sorts of levels, and most local councils as well as gyms and local tennis clubs do coaching courses. Once you've learned the fundamentals of the game there are lots of places to play: parks, leisure centres and clubs.

Up-boarding

I've called it 'up-boarding' rather than 'sup-boarding' because sup-boarding is stand-up boarding, and a lot of people never quite get to the stage where they can stand up on the boards. But you'll get plenty of exercise even if you're sitting on a board paddling out into a lake, a river or at sea. Boarding is basically a surfboard on which you stand/sit or lie and paddle with an oar.

If you live near a river, there'll be lots of sailing clubs along the river, many of which will have other water activity equipment. This is something a lot of people try when they're on holiday, but there is no reason you can't continue when you get back home, if you live near a reservoir or river, or indeed are near the sea. It actually uses a lot of the core muscles that hold you upright while you're standing on the board, and gives you a thorough workout while you desperately try to stay on the thing.

Volleyball

Most local councils run volleyball sessions because it's relatively easy to organise them: you just need a space, some friends and a net. You can put up a net in the garden, or on the beach, and test yourself with the sport. There are lots of clubs, leagues, teams and classes all over the country, most parks have volleyball leagues in them, and it's a lovely sport to meet new people and get running around in the sunshine.

Weightlifting

Yep, I know what you're thinking, and I thought that too: WHY THE HELL IN GOD'S NAME WOULD I DO WEIGHTLIFTING. I WANT TO LOOK SMALLER NOT BIGGER. But weightlifting is a fantastic way to burn fat because it builds muscle and the more muscle you have, the more fat you'll burn. If you incorporate weight training into your exercise routine, you'll be burning fat hours after you've stopped training. You won't look like Arnold Schwarzenegger but you will find it easier to shed the pounds and tone up, rather than just doing aerobic exercise alone.

X-RATED behaviour

I'm not going to go into any details about this in such polite, sophisticated company, but – it burns loads of calories, so get to it.

YOGA

You've only got to look at the people going into a yoga class to realise that it's doing some good. It's worth attending a class for a few sessions to learn directly from an instructor who will correct your form and check you are doing the basics correctly, then there are tons of videos, online classes and books to help you improve.

Zumba

This is my favourite. It's a real feel-good class that will have you smiling and jogging to the music as you wave your arms to the Latin beat. It doesn't matter whether you're moving in time to the music or in sync with everyone else...just dance, smile and enjoy yourself. You'll never look back.

EXERCISING AT HOME

Now then. For some people, the idea of going out and doing a fitness class is just too much, and they don't feel they are fit enough to go along to netball or swimming lessons. So, if you want to get your fitness levels up quietly at home before starting to train in public, here is an A–Z of exercises you can do without leaving the comfort of your own home.

- **Arm circles:** Stand up and stretch your arms out to the side, palms facing down. Make small circles with your outstretched arms. Try 20 small circles, then 20 medium, then 20 large, then 20 medium, then 20 small again. It is much tougher than it looks, so if you haven't done much exercise before, start with five of each and work up. Repeat in the opposite direction for the same amount of time.

- **Burpees:** This is an advanced exercise so take it easy, but it's worth trying one to see how you get on. From a standing position, bend down to touch the floor and kick your feet back so you are in a push-up position. If you are doing full burpees, do a push-up, if not, just jump or walk your feet back in. Then jump into the air when you stand up (if you can) reaching your arms overhead.
- **Calf raises:** Stand up straight on the edge of a step with your heels hanging over the edge. Rest your hands against a wall or a sturdy object for balance. Raise your heels a few inches above the edge of the step until you're on your tiptoes. Hold the position for a few seconds and then lower your heels below the step.
- **Donkey kicks:** Get onto all fours and look straight ahead. With your knee bent at a 90-degree angle, lift a leg into the air until your knee is as high as your torso and then lower the leg back down. Switch legs.
- **Elbow plank:** This is just the process of doing a plank on your elbows. A plank is when you get into the press-up position and hold it. This one, obviously, involves being on elbows instead of hands. You have to squeeze your abs and keep your neck and spine in a straight line, looking at a spot just in front of your hands.
- **Front leg raises:** Stand next to a chair and hold it with one hand. With hips and legs as straight as possible, kick one leg in front, and then

kicking behind in a swift motion as you come back down. Repeat on the other leg.

- **Glute bridges:** Lay on your back, knees in the air and feet on the mat. Slowly raise your hips into the air as high as you can, squeeze your glutes and come back down.
- **High knees:** From a standing position, quickly jump from one foot to the other, lifting each knee to hip height, like a running motion.
- **Inchworms:** From a standing position, stretch down and bring your hands to your feet. Slowly walk your hands out until you are in a push-up position. Slowly walk your feet to your hands. Note – this is quite tough!
- **Jumping jacks:** From a standing position, slightly bend your knees and jump up, making a star shape in the air with your arms and legs, then close them and land back down. If you find this tough, jump out from legs apart to legs together, then jump out and in again.
- **Knee-to-elbow planks:** Just like the normal plank from sit-up position, lift and bend your right leg, bringing your right knee to your right elbow. Switch legs.
- **Lunges:** From a standing position, step forward with one leg, lowering hips until both knees are at a 90-degree angle. Be sure your front knee is directly above your ankle and the other knee isn't touching the floor. Push back up to the starting position and repeat on the other side.

- **Mountain climbers:** Start in a push-up position. Lift your right foot off the floor and raise your knee as close to your chest as you can, then back into your original position, repeat with your left leg, almost like you're running on the floor.
- **Narrow squats:** Stand straight with your feet as close together as possible, knees touching and your arms at your sides. Lower your body by pushing your hips back and bending your knees. As you lower your body, push through your heels and raise your arms in front of you. Pause then lift back into starting position.
- **Overhead arm pulls:** Stand up straight and place your left hand behind your head. Grasp above your left elbow with your right hand and pull to the right, pulling your body over to the right. Hold this position for five seconds. Return to the starting position and repeat with the opposite arm.
- **Push-ups:** Start in the press-up position, then drop your knees to the floor if you need to and lower your body until your chest almost touches the floor. Keep your back flat, and push back up.
- **Quadraplex:** On hands and knees, raise one arm, straight forward, while simultaneously raising your opposite leg straight back. Return to starting position and repeat using the other arm and leg.

- **Reverse crunches:** Lie on your back. Lift your legs with your knees bent so they form a 90-degree angle with the floor. While inhaling, move your legs towards your chest as you roll your pelvis backwards and raise your hips off the floor. Exhale when you move back to the starting position.
- **Shoulder taps:** Start in a push-up position with your feet hip-width apart, hands under your shoulders. Lightly tap your left shoulder with your right hand. Repeat with the opposite hand.
- **Triceps dips:** Start by sitting down (an excellent start, I think you will all agree). Then place your hands next to you on a chair and move your feet out in front of you. Inch forward so your hips are off the chair, bend your arms and dip down. Return to original position and repeat.
- **Upright rows:** Use weights (cans of beans or bags of sugar will do) or a resistance band. From a standing position, hold the weights at your side, or put one end of the resistance band under your feet, and grip the other end with both hands. Keeping your arms as close to your torso as possible, lift your arms with elbows first until you can't go any higher. Your elbows should be about as high as your face. Palms should face inwards.
- **V-sits:** Lie on your back with arms stretched out. Raise your legs and chest to form a 'V' shape, bracing your hands on the floor. Return to starting position. Note – this is hard!

- **Wall sits:** Stand with your back against a wall and your feet about two feet in front of you. Slide down until your knees are at a 90-degree angle. Hold in place, keeping as tight as possible.
- **X-punches:** Lie on your back with your knees bent and feet flat on the floor. Put your hands in a fighting position. Perform a standard sit-up while making four cross-body punches on the way up, then go back down slowly.
- **YTMs:** Using weights or a resistance band, create the letters 'Y', 'T', 'M' with your arms.
- **Zigzag hops:** Pretending there is a straight line in front of you, jump forward and side-to-side (zigzag) for as far as you can. If you run out of space, turn around and come back again.

So, there you go. Don't worry about looking like a sweaty mess. Remember what I keep saying - don't worry about what other people are thinking (I swear they are all too worried about what they look like to even notice whether you look unfit and out of breath). Go and throw a little fun and exercise into your life. It's something you will never regret doing. If you are going to start by exercising on your own at home, be careful! Look through the exercises above and try working through any that appeal to you very slowly and gently so as not to injure yourself. If you have done no exercise for a long time, please see a doctor first.

SECTION EIGHT

EATING

FAT PEOPLE NEED TO EAT TOO

OK, so eating may seem like a really odd subject to tackle in a handbook for overweight people. After all, one could sensibly argue that if there's one thing that fat people don't need advice on it is eating. They know how to do that very well, thank you very much.

But this is a guide to the complexities and awkwardness that arise out of eating. The issues that fat people have and the opprobrium they attract when doing something that everyone does; something everyone has to do in order to survive.

These complexities can range from not eating anything at all in a desperate and flawed attempt to lose weight quickly, to eating everything you can get your hands on in order to fill yourself quickly. Whichever one you're doing, it's all part of the same problem of using food to alter your mood rather than fill your stomach. I've eaten food from the bin, feeling overwhelmed with desire to retrieve the cake, crisps or takeaway that I've disposed of, and eat it hungrily.

But there's nothing 'food hungry' about this behaviour. It's got nothing to do with physical hunger, and everything to do with emotional hunger. It's about knowing the food is there, and feeling a 'need' to consume it because it will make you feel momentarily happy. I repeat: it's not about being food hungry.

I think that's what people who eat regularly and without compulsions really struggle to understand... They don't have the manic feelings of needy desperation around food. They don't get the same whole-body thrill from ordering a huge takeaway and eating the whole damn thing yourself. The wonderful anticipation when you know you've ordered a massive amount of food. The excitement is overwhelming. The tearing into the salty bag of chips and pushing huge handfuls into your mouth as if there's some sort of race to consume as much as you can before even unloading the rest of the order. The anticipation of food and the first mouthfuls are mind-bending. Better, perhaps, than the reality of actually eating it all, feeling completely stuffed afterwards and feeling wracked with guilt the next day.

Guilt features quite a lot in my eating and that of my friends. Guilt is a strong feeling. And we all know what to do with strong feelings, don't we? Bury them. Eat loads and loads to block out the feelings. That's the vicious cycle. You get exactly the same cycle with gambling, alcohol, drugs and any other obsession. But food is harder, as I keep saying in this book, because you have to face it every day.

Then there's the lying... When you don't eat all that much in public and you eat tons when you are alone.

Lying to yourself. Plenty of times I've bought jumbo bags full of crisps for my son knowing full well that I will eat them all myself. My son's not keen on crisps. Yet in that moment, in the shop, I can easily convince myself that I am buying them for him, and him alone.

I remember when I was at university, I had a friend who was always getting herself into trouble with money; she had a voracious appetite for new clothes and no conceivable way of paying for them. I remember clearly when she was called in to see the back manager and they discussed her cavalier attitude towards money and how things had to change. When she got back to the flat, she was worried about how to solve her problem.

"I treated myself to make myself feel better," she declared, holding up a Topshop bag. "Look what I bought!"

Her reaction to debt problems was to spend more money. My reaction to being overweight is to eat more food. If you have a problem with something, you have a problem with it. It doesn't matter whether that 'it' is over-spending, overeating, gambling, doing drugs or being oversexed.

The problems associated with eating are exacerbated and highlighted when it comes to dining out. Basically, this is taking your 'problem' out and displaying it to the world. Many of us eat alone, certainly binge alone. No one who is overweight wants to go to a restaurant and order something fattening, then feel guilty for eating it in public. There's too much guilt already…we don't need any more. Then there's the small seating areas, the squeezing between tables to get to the loos, and the realisation that everyone else has stopped eating, and left something on their plate and you've just wolfed it all down. Eating out is a minefield, as I explore further in the next chapter.

THE TOP FIVE HORRORS OF EATING OUT

1. Thin friends

Obviously not all thin friends, but top of the list I suggest we put thin friends who order extra slimline salads (i.e.: nothing but bloody lettuce) while you're tucking into a burger, then talk endlessly about how fat they are and how much weight they need to lose, even though they are clearly no wider than your arm. These people are the devil personified. Really. I know you're thinking that's quite an extreme statement to make, but if you weigh less than 120 lbs and when you lift up your top to show us all your bulging midriff there's nothing there, you're not going to be very popular. You wanna see a bulging midriff? Do you? Well, take a look at this (except – don't do that last bit – not good for self-esteem).

2. The judgement

There's that moment when you sense the judgement in the eyes of waiters when you order fries. That subtle eyebrow raise, that half smile... Interestingly, this look is much the same as the look you get from shop assistants when you're a size 20 and you pick up a size 12 dress. Do they all go to the same training school, or something?

3. Banquettes that are too small

You arrive at the restaurant with your friends. You've booked a table for four and the waitress leads you through the restaurant to it, but she's leading you to...a booth. Oh no. It's a small booth, and as you're approaching it you know there is no way you are going to squeeze into it. But you have to go to it anyway because – what else can you do? Stop dead in your tracks and shout, "No, I'm too fat." Sometimes you can squeeze yourself in, and you tell everyone you're fine but your legs are jammed and uncomfortable and you can hardly move and you can't wait for the whole thing to be over. Other times you can't fit in and there's an embarrassing pause while you have to be relocated.

4. Tiny bathroom

Sometimes the bathroom cubicles are so small that you have to reverse in to have any chance of being able to use the thing. They are horrible for everyone to use, I imagine, but I can say with some authority that they are impossible for those who are carrying a little extra weight. If there's a disabled loo, I'll tend to go in there, and hope to goodness that someone in a wheelchair doesn't come along when I'm in there.

. . .

5. Hide the fat guy

In my research for this book, I talked to a lovely woman at Weight Watchers who told me of the time she went to the hairdressers and was moved to the back of the salon so she couldn't be seen by people passing the window. She was mortified, but realised straight away what was going on: they didn't want someone overweight linked with the salon in the eyes of passers-by. It's why designers only make small garments as sample sizes: because they don't want larger people in their clothes.

The lady from Weight Watchers explained that the 'hide the inappropriate customers' technique was used most frequently in restaurants. So, someone will turn up at a restaurant for dinner and see there are plenty of empty tables: excellent. They are told to go to the bar and wait while they prepare a table, but then people walking in are seated at the spare tables in front of them. Then, when a table becomes available at which they cannot not be easily seen, in the back corner, tucked away, they are taken to it.

It happens frequently because restaurants want to project themselves as somewhere lovely to spend an evening, and they worry that people will see them as the first step on the path to gluttony if there are lots of overweight people there. One restaurant owner told me that they don't like overweight people on show in the restaurant in the same way that a landlord would not want drunks on show in his pub. I tried to explain that it was a very different scenario. "People *need* to eat. Eating is not bad." But all I got was a shrug.

If you experience discrimination in restaurants, do call it out. If you don't want to say anything there and then, a letter through the door the next day threatening a bad review, or just going for it and writing a bad review are valid responses.

SECTION NINE

CLOTHES

CHOOSING CLOTHES

Your skin may be as smooth as marble and your hair may glisten with the shine of a thousand suns. You may have a face more beautiful than Cleopatra's, but – my God – if you're more than a few pounds overweight, trying to look good becomes a conundrum more complex than any mathematical formula.

It's clothes, you see: they're a nightmare.

You do all the usual worrying… Will I look the way I want to; will I be comfortable; do I look decent without looking too stuffy? Are my boobs showing, is too much leg showing? Too little leg? Too little boob?

But if you are fat, you have a whole other layer of thought processes on top: do I look too fat? Is everything hidden? Is it obvious that I'm dressing to hide everything?

And, of course: where can I go to buy nice clothes that will fit me and make me feel good? Where do they stock clothes in larger sizes? So many questions and not too many easy answers (but I'll try).

. . .

1. The sizing in shops

This is one of the most life-sucking, morale-draining problems of being overweight. If you go into a standard store, you'll be lucky if the clothes are on offer in anything above a 16. Now this is bonkers for so many reasons.

First, a size 16 is the average size in the UK, so it should be the middle of the range, not the top of the range. Second, these are the sizes that everyone wants. You've only got to go to the sales and see what's left behind to see very clearly that it's the size 8s and 10s that are left on the rack. I put a load of clothes on eBay recently – for me and for a friend. The size 16 and 18 clothes went immediately. The size 8 clothes never sold. Size 8 is very small by today's standards, but manufacturers and retail outlets blithely storm ahead as if there are as many size 8s around as size 16s. This all goes to reinforce the notion that if you are a size 16, you are 'outsized'. You're not.

2. Changing rooms

These truly are the bane of the overweight woman. Small, harshly lit and full of mirrors. I swear, every time I go into one, I feel like I'm having an anxiety dream. It's not only that it's quite unnerving to see yourself from every direction while you remove your elasticated waist jeans, it's also the fact that despite there being mirrors everywhere, paradoxically, it's hard to see yourself properly when you're standing that close up to them, so you have to take a step back out of the cubicle to look properly in the mirror. When the changing room is situated in the corner of the shop, you're standing in the shop, being watched by all the shoppers while you examine whether the new item covers your muffin top properly. Really, it's not for the faint-hearted.

3. When the outfit is smaller than you thought it would be

Ah, but there is nothing more horrific in the whole world of shopping than when you take an item into the changing room, thinking you'll fit into it, then when you're halfway into it, you realise it doesn't fit you. The panic is like that awful feeling you get when you've got your head or hand stuck in something, and a horrible panic rips through you as you consider that you might never extricate yourself and will be in there forever.

4. Plus-size shops

So, you think to yourself, I don't want to have to worry about whether they've got clothes to fit me, and I certainly don't want to be stuck in a size 16 dress that I can't get off, so I will go to a plus-size shop and there I will find a whole array of clothes, all of which fit me. Perfect.

So, you head for the plus-size shop on the other side of town. And the good news is that – indeed – everything in there fits you. To your delight you try on several outfits that are too big, and you sing with joy at the feeling of baggy tops, and skirts which fall off. You feel petite, feminine and alluring. The only problem is...the clothes. They are so boring.

Even in the plus-size sections of standard shops, check out the colours on offer: a sea of neutral-coloured outfits. Perfect if you're 97 and moving into an old people's home, or if you are a police officer who needs to replace her navy knee-length skirt, but if you fancy funky designs, pretty colours and sumptuous fabrics you're in the wrong place. No vibrant colours or unusual cuts. Is that because most overweight people have requested plain clothes? Perhaps they want to go undercover on the beach in all that beige? It seems a shame though. It would be nice to have the clothes that everyone else is wearing in larger sizes. That's not too much to ask, is it?

5. It's all about the kaftans

Now, there's nothing wrong with kaftans. They can look lovely, but surely they're not the only thing that those designing for the overweight can create? There must be other things, for heaven's sake. Outsize clothing is 90% kaftan. So many kaftans. If you manage to find something that isn't kaftan in shape, the pattern will be the sort of thing never seen on 'normal' clothing. Most things are covered in flowers. Flowers are lovely...in the garden or in a vase, but not all over a polyester blouse.

6. Online shopping

Online shopping. Brilliant. You get to avoid changing rooms, other shoppers and judgey shop assistants. Also, there's a much wider range of sizes on sale. Many sites for larger sizes go up to a British size 32. You're never going to find that in a standard branch of Marks and Spencer, but you just might online. Nike are even getting in on the act now, launching a plus-size line (finally). You can buy things and try them on at home and send them back if they make you look like a hippo.

7. Forward buying

We all need to stop this. We need to stop buying things that aren't the right size or style for now, but are bought "for when I lose weight". Shop for what makes you look and feel good right now. Don't worry about the future... If you lose weight, all well and good. But right now, in this moment, buy clothing that is comfortable, flattering and makes you happy today and that you want to wear tomorrow.

ARE YOU INVISIBLE?

It's a truth, acknowledged by everyone who is overweight, that the bigger you are, the less the assistants in shops appear to be able to see you. It's bizarre, I know, but we all know it to be true. Now researchers have stepped in to confirm our suspicions. It wasn't that you *felt* that you were being ignored in that store: you were being ignored.

Jeannine A. Gailey, writer of *The Hyper(in)visible Fat Woman,* discusses the paradox at the centre of every fat woman's experience of shopping: you are the biggest in the room but no one appears to be able to see you. She quotes a research project, in which researchers called Casper and Moore (2009) looked at women who were shopping, and saw that slimmer women were offered assistance more quickly than women who were fat. There was a real discrepancy in attention.

"Using participant observation, the couple examined the treatment of fat customers and clothing options available for plus size women in various types of popular women's clothing stores." The sales clerks ignored fat women regularly, in contrast they greeted, helped and tended to thinner customers. Fat women talked of feeling "out of place" in retail stores.

As part of their research they spoke to a woman called Rochelle, who said: "During my teenage years, when I was not as heavy, people spoke to me in public, they were nice. You could get friendly conversation out of a cashier or a passer-by. During my heaviest and my late 20s, I was like, I know I'm the biggest person in here, yet nobody actually sees me. It's almost like being invisible: people look right through you. Cashiers don't even look at you in your eyes when they speak to you. Now, at my heaviest, I'm just dismissed before I can even make my presence known."

It's interesting to hear Rochelle's views because she has witnessed first-hand the difference in the way people treated her when she was not heavy and when she was at her heaviest. Rochelle became more invisible the more weight she put on, not because people couldn't see her, but because they were choosing to dismiss her. Therefore, she was simultaneously seen and ignored.

Rochelle was not alone. In the 74 interviews Casper and Moore conducted for their research, they saw time and again that fat women were being ignored.

A woman called Evelyn (32) said:

"I walked into a store and an assistant asked me whether she could help me find anything. She was quite dismissive of me in her tone, as if she didn't really want to help me but thought she ought to. I asked for help, anyway: I explained that I was looking for a strapless bra to go with my bridesmaid's dress.

"She turned to her co-workers and said: 'Oh, I don't think we have anything in her size.'

"'I don't think we do,' said the other woman, then they began talking among themselves."

Evelyn described how she stood there, open-mouthed and shocked that the assistant hadn't even addressed her to answer the question. "She spoke to her co-worker, not to me. It was like I didn't matter. They expected me to overhear the reply and leave the shop so they could carry on chatting."

This is a bit like the situation that disabled people describe, where someone will ask an able-bodied person with them: "Does he take sugar?" rather than addressing the comment to them directly.

I remember going to see a Shakespeare play outdoors at a beautiful park near where I live a few years ago. The tickets had been bought by a friend who is in a wheelchair. When we arrived, my friend went to the front, and said hello to the ticket collector, who immediately turned to me and asked me for our tickets.

"He has them," I said, pointing to my friend who was pulling them out of his jacket pocket.

"Oh, OK," said the ticket collector, keeping his hand out, directed at me. It meant that my friend had to hand the tickets to me for me to hand them to the ticket inspector. He clearly didn't believe that our friend in a wheelchair had the capacity to show him the tickets.

Where does this come from? And is this the same theory that leaves overweight people feeling ignored, and not communicated with in shops? Do people think that overweight people are inherently less able to communicate in shops, are they worried about talking to them because they know they only have a small collection of plus-size clothing and none of the 'normal' clothes will fit them, or is it something deeper, more primitive that causes this reaction? It's impossible to know without much more research.

SECTION TEN

WEIGHT-LOSS STORIES AND STUDIES

PEOPLE WHO HAVE LOST WEIGHT EXPLAIN HOW THEY DID IT

Now, I wasn't sure whether to include this section in the book. This is a handbook which urges you to feel good about yourself, challenge stereotypes and be happy the way you are. There's no need to be thin, and there is no need to feel that you are somehow 'less than' if you are overweight. But, at the same time, many reading this book will want to lose weight. Many will have tried and not succeeded.

For those people, here are some snapshots of people who have successfully lost weight and kept it off. This section is to show you that you CAN lose weight if you want to. You can do it healthily and successfully. I have featured 20 people and they all answer two questions: what happened to make you want to lose weight? And how did you go about doing it?

There are men and women included, and there's a wide age range: from 20 to 60 years old. I hope you find their stories uplifting, and that they help you feel positive about yourself, and your ability to shift a few pounds ***if*** you want to.

KATIE: lost 130 lbs

Katie was 22 years old and 270 lbs and knew she was overweight, but it wasn't until her doctor told her that she was morbidly obese and putting her life in danger, that she decided to lose weight.

WHAT HAPPENED to make her want to lose weight?

"I did it because my life was at risk: that was the reason. I wanted to look better and fit into nice clothes, but it was the realisation that it was affecting my health that made me take action."

HOW DID SHE LOSE IT?

To lose weight and get healthy, Katie began tracking her food intake and became more aware of how much sugar, fat and carbohydrates she was consuming. But the biggest change in her lifestyle came from discovering a love of fitness. Now she does cardio five days a week and strength training two to three days a week, and has trained to be a personal trainer. "You start to feel that serotonin and dopamine and all that from exercise. I used that as the outlet for stress, anxiety, depression. That made a huge difference."

. . .

Barbara: lost 226 lbs

Barbara spent most of her life overweight. She was obese as a child, and by the time she was 25, she weighed in at 376 lbs. "I had no one else to blame but myself," she says.

What happened to make her want to lose weight?

Signing up for a weight-loss programme was what changed her mind set and allowed her to lose weight.

How did she lose it?

Over 15 weeks she dropped 100 lbs, thanks to a personal trainer, nutrition coaching and regular boot-camp classes. But the hardest part, she says, was when that ended and she had to do it on her own. "I had to understand that this was no longer a diet, and that it had to become my lifestyle," she says. Barbara kept up her daily workouts and nutrition plan, and just 10 months after starting the programme, she was down to 175 lbs.

Marsha: lost 155 lbs

As the single mother of a new born, Marsha found it extremely difficult to cope. She had to take a lower-paying job with flexible hours so she could take care of her daughter. She fed her daughter with the best, most healthy food she could afford, while she ate fried food to make herself feel better.

"I was stressed out and had the baby blues. My

daughter would be asleep and I would be crying, eating chocolate and drinking fizzy drinks. I would buy foods that I knew were bad, but they gave me comfort at the time." Her weight climbed, and by the time her little girl turned five, Marsha weighed 290 lbs, had developed high blood pressure and was pre-diabetic.

What happened to make her want to lose weight?

It was her daughter, in the end, who persuaded her to lose weight. "I would have headaches from the food and she would say, 'I'm really, really worried about you.' I realized that my health was connected to her wellbeing."

How did she do it?

She decided to begin exercising, by taking kickboxing classes and switching to a healthier diet, drinking green smoothies and prioritising lean proteins like fish, chicken and eggs. That, along with a newfound love of weightlifting, helped her lose 155 lbs. "My daughter saved my life."

Kimberly: lost 109 lbs

When Kimberly, 34, decided to make a change and lose weight, she was at an all-time low; she had recently suffered a miscarriage, her childhood pet had died and a broken ankle left her unable to walk on her own.

What happened to make her want to lose weight?

"My health was suffering," said Kimberly. She had high blood pressure and frequent migraines, and her doctor thought that losing some of her 239 lbs would help.

How did she do it?

She decided to get herself a nutritionist to advise her, and she immediately had success, dropping 10 lbs in the first week and around 2.5 lbs every week after. Four years later, she's healthier and 109 lbs lighter.

"I currently weigh 130 lb and I no longer have to take any medication for my blood pressure."

Jennifer: lost 76 lbs

Jennifer was always tired and had trouble keeping up with her young son, so she went to see her doctor.

What happened to make her want to lose weight?

When her doctor told her that her fast-food habit may be to blame she realised it was time to make a change. "In reality, I had just given up on myself. Everybody became more important than I did and fast food became my way of life. It was fast. It was easy."

How did she lose it?

Jennifer cut out greasy food and substituted it with meal replacement shakes. She also got active. Now she exercises regularly and can keep pace with her 13-year-old son. "The challenge itself is to feel better about yourself, to be the best version of you, whoever you are."

KIRSTEN: lost 133 lbs

When Kirsten "became sedentary" in college, she piled on the weight, and it only got worse. She met a guy who loved food as much as she did, and they would order takeaways every night: pizzas, cheeseburgers and fries, and rarely cook. "I was part of a group that drank a lot, and with a partner who ate a lot, so I did that too."

WHAT HAPPENED to make her want to lose weight?

Five years into their relationship, her boyfriend said he had feelings for someone else.

She broke up with him, moved out of their apartment and started a new job. It was the clean slate she needed to lose weight for good. "I literally got rid of every excuse that I've ever had," she says.

HOW DID SHE DO IT?

Kirsten realised she couldn't do it on her own and joined Jenny Craig. Over the next two years she lost 133 lbs (nearly half her size) with the pre-made meals and a newfound love for group fitness classes and weight training.

MARY JANE: lost 135 lbs

When Mary got engaged in 2016, she was thrilled to marry her long-time boyfriend but she knew that their eating habits were dangerous.

What happened to make her want to lose weight?

After six years of fast-food dinners and minimal exercise, she weighed 281 lbs and was having knee problems. She was dreading buying a wedding dress at her size, and knew things had to change.

How did she do it?

Along with her fiancé, she started tracking her meals and calories with the LoseIt! app. She dropped 75 lbs in a year, and started incorporating exercise into her routine. By her wedding day in November 2018, she had lost 135 lbs and was able to buy the dress of her dreams in a size 8.

Randi: lost 80 lbs

Randi was a 'chubby' child, but it never bothered her, until she left work and couldn't find a job she loved. She started drowning her sorrows in boozy brunches and fast food.

What happened to make her want to lose weight?

"I was getting heavier and heavier and hit 240 lbs. I started to notice that my confidence was going down, and I wasn't motivated to do anything. It started to click that if I didn't change my life that it would just get worse and worse."

How did she do it?

She found a gym class at her local YMCA that she loved. Within a few months she dropped 20 lbs, which inspired her to keep going. She began cooking healthier meals and started doing Kayla Itsines' popular workout plan.

Tara: lost 122 lbs

Tara says that being bullied at school meant she developed a hatred of eating in front of her schoolmates. "I'd starve myself until 4 pm, then go home and eat 'anything and everything' in sight," she confessed. Her weight kept crawling up, eventually reaching 260 lbs.

What happened to make her want to lose weight?

"I'd always been fat, but then I was diagnosed with rheumatoid arthritis, and in so much pain that I wasn't able to hug my children. I decided there and then to change my lifestyle."

How did she do it?

She went to high-intensity interval training workouts and adopted a 'clean-eating' diet. "Nowadays I get all the hugs I can and they can even wrap their little hands all the way around my body."

ALAN: lost 317 lbs

At 538 lbs, Alan knew his relationship with food was unhealthy. He ate at fast-food restaurants all the time and consumed around 6,000 calories.

"My weight was affecting my life: I couldn't stand up in a shower for ten minutes. Even doing dishes and cooking required a chair."

WHAT HAPPENED to make him want to lose weight?

It was coming home to his three- and five-year-old daughters that pushed him to lose weight. He hated that they saw him so weak and unable to perform the simplest of tasks.

HOW DID HE DO IT?

He committed himself to diet and exercise and signed up for Optavia, a coach-based wellness programme. In just 18 months, he slimmed down to 221 lbs.

SHARRON: lost 151 lbs

At nine years old, Sharron started sneaking pieces of cake from the fridge. The urge to hide her food continued through to her adult life, when she would often order entire meals from two fast-food restaurants at a time and eat them in her car. "I hid my worst eating habits — overeating or bingeing to the point of being in pain."

WHAT HAPPENED to make her want to lose weight?

"In 2011 I reached my highest weight ever. It was a shock to me how heavy I had become."

HOW DID SHE DO IT?

"I signed up for WW, then called Weight Watchers, and it changed my mindset." She ditched the fast-food meals and began eating more fruits and vegetables, she also began walking and doing daily light exercise. Four years later, she had slimmed down from 291 lbs to 140 lbs.

JANINE: lost 145 lbs

WHAT HAPPENED to make her want to lose weight?

When Janine tried on the wedding dress she had ordered online, she knew she had to make a change. She weighed 299 lbs and didn't look the way she wanted to. She vowed to lose 100 lbs by her wedding a year later.

HOW DID SHE DO IT?

She started by making healthier meals, and set a daily step goal on her Fitbit. Once the pounds started to fall off, she joined a local kickboxing gym and supplemented her walking with high-intensity cardio classes. Five days before her wedding, she met her goal.

JENNA: lost 140 lbs

Jenna always considered herself to be fit and athletic. But after she became pregnant with her daughter in 2000, she continued to put on weight.

"I started trying quick fixes and that's when the vicious crash diets really started. A few of them worked but just for a minute. I would lose 20 lbs and gain back double."

WHAT HAPPENED to make her want to lose weight?

When her weight hit 270 lbs, she considered getting weight-loss surgery, but first wanted to try her hand at losing it naturally.

HOW DID SHE DO IT?

She adopted a high-protein, low-carb diet and began exercising. She reached her goal weight of 130 lbs in 2014.

"It's never too late to change your life no matter how long you've been stuck."

NICOLE: lost 204 lbs

Nicole grew up thinking that fast food was the only food.

"I would consume one Big Mac, one McChicken and

one large order of French fries," she said, and would sometimes add another medium order of fries. At her heaviest, Nicole weighed 350 lbs.

What happened to make her want to lose weight?

When she was unpacking after moving back to her hometown, she saw an advert for a '21 Day Fix', a programme that combined portion-controlled eating with 30 minutes of exercise per day. She decided to try it out, and slowly but surely, she slimmed down.

How did she do it?

She just followed exactly what they told her to do – she stuck to a diet of vegetables and small portions of carbs. Nothing was off limits and she still allowed herself desserts or small bags of chips. By the end of 2017 she had reached her goal weight of 146 lbs.

Holly: lost 162 lbs

Holly was always 'chubby' as a kid, but it wasn't until high school that she became an emotional eater.

What happened to make her want to lose weight?

At 48 years old, Holly went to the doctor's weighing 308 lbs, and was told that she was 'morbidly obese'. Her doctor suggested options for how she could slim down.

That day, she set a goal to lose half her weight by her 50th birthday.

How did she do it?

She began a high-fat, moderate-protein, low-carb diet and tracked her goals, eating habits and exercise in an app called 'Lose It'. Now, at 146 lbs, Holly is able to cycle 29 miles and has run her first half marathon.

Scott: lost 193 lbs

Scott attempted his first diet at 19, when he weighed 438 lbs. He was in college and often drank alcohol and finished the night off with fatty foods such as chicken wings or sweets and chips. "I wouldn't think twice about eating two whole pizzas."

What happened to make him want to lose weight?

In 2015 that he decided to make a lifestyle change since he couldn't catch up with his toddler. "I tried to run after her but couldn't get above a moderate walk. All I could do was watch her."

How did he do it?

He started doing a digital weight-loss programme that provides coaches, support groups and helps set daily goals for diet and exercise. He stuck to a strict 800–900 calorie diet and went running or walking every day. Now, at 170 lbs, he is able to run 5Ks with his daughters.

CARA: lost 95 lbs

Cara had worked out regularly in high school but when she went away to college, her routine changed. "I became complacent and the weight just kept piling on and I just hung out with my friends and ate a lot of food I shouldn't have eaten."

WHAT HAPPENED to make her want to lose weight?

She started experiencing panic attacks after having her second child, and she knew she needed to make a major life change to be healthier for her family.

HOW DID SHE DO IT?

Cara discovered Daily Burn, a health and fitness app that provided workout videos and nutritional guidance.

She did the app's 30-minute workouts in her living room three to four times a week while her kids were nearby.

"Since they were quick workouts, I could fit them in whenever I had time with little ones running around," she said.

She now weighs 185 lbs. "It's really boosted my confidence and my comfort level to just try everything and live a more active, healthy lifestyle."

. . .

Kevin: lost 125 lbs

Kevin weighed 300 lbs by consuming "a diet full of bread, pasta and chips." Then, one day, everything changed.

What happened to make him want to lose weight?

"My sister was diagnosed with an aggressive, rare form of cancer, I decided to change my life. How could I literally eat myself to death while my poor sister was fighting for her life?"

How did he do it?

He eliminated processed carbohydrates and stuck to fruits, vegetables, nuts, chicken, turkey, fish, eggs, non-fat Greek yogurt, olive oil, balsamic vinegar, and non-caloric spices and seasoning. He also only ate between 12 pm to 8 pm every day. Outside of that window he allowed himself black tea, black coffee and water.

Anne: lost 107 lbs

When Anne fell pregnant, she "used it as an excuse" to indulge in comfort foods. "I assumed it would all fall off pretty easily after the baby was born," she said. But after giving birth to her son, Anne continued her poor eating habits and put on more weight.

What happened to make her want to lose weight?

"There was no one thing...no moment in which I saw the light, just a gradual realisation that I couldn't go on like this."

How did she do it?

Anne eventually signed up with a personal trainer at the gym, and started training two to three times a week in weightlifting, plyometrics and boxing. She ditched her processed, carb-heavy meals for lean proteins, healthy fats and vegetables. A year later, she had dropped 100 lbs and started powerlifting competitively. She even became a trainer at the gym that helped her lose weight.

Rachel: lost 121 lbs

Rachel says that she was always big, and never let it get her down. In school she hit 200 lbs but it didn't bother her. She continued to gain weight and reached her highest, 291 lbs, after the birth of her daughter in 2007.

What happened to make her want to lose weight?

In January 2017, she got a wake-up call. Her daughter, now 10 years old, said a classmate had had said: "Your mum's fat."

"At that moment it hit me that she's suffering, and she's being picked on or laughed at because of my laziness or my unhealthy choices. That definitely inspired me."

. . .

How did she do it?

She cut out fast food and soda and started doing daily three-mile walks around the lake in her town. Less than 12 months later, she reached her goal. "I cried," she says. "It was an amazing feeling."

HOW TO AVOID A RELAPSE

Why do so many people relapse?

This is the crucial question. We've all done it. You lose weight, feel thrilled at your accomplishment but end up relapsing and regaining the weight you have lost. I know I have done it. You put all the effort in the world into losing it, but then when you drift back to your 'normal' life, you put it on and it's maddening. If you're not careful this throws you into a mad cycle of losing weight, gaining weight and losing it again – yoyo dieting as it's called.

But why on earth do we do it? Research by Sirpa Sarlio-Lahteenkorva, reported in the 'European Journal of Public Health', set out to look at this, and to work out why people who lose weight end up relapsing.

The study

In total, 90 subjects were involved in the study, all from the Helsinki area (Finland). These included 71 obese employees from a local hospital and 19 obese persons recruited from a private clinic. They had all applied for weight-loss treatment having previously lost weight and put it back on again. They were told the in-depth interview was part of their application.

Most of the subjects were middle-aged females from lower level white-collar backgrounds, but the range of ages actually went from 21 to 66 years. All subjects were obese with a mean body mass index (BMI) of 36 (severe obesity), 22% of the subjects could be classified as morbidly obese (BMI of over 40).

Through the respondents' answers, the researchers showed that there were three main reasons why people relapsed after weight-loss. These can be summarised as:

- Lack of supervision
- Anti-dieting values
- Unrealistically high hopes connected to weight loss

So, in other words – some people found it extraordinarily difficult to lose weight unless they were being supervised by someone and told what to eat, others hated dieting and found it negatively affected their lives so didn't want to have to do it all the time, and others didn't feel as wonderful as they thought they would when they lost weight. Their lives weren't transformed so they found it easy to stop dieting and put the weight on again.

Let's look at the three reasons in more detail:

. . .

Lack of supervision

This was a reason mentioned by many of the respondents. They said things like: "Dieting is so easy when you have good instructions, but somehow I always gain it back when I leave the programme." The researchers said that the subjects knew a lot about weight management and many demonstrated excellent nutritional knowledge but, nevertheless, wanted to have outside control and clear instructions. They felt they needed to be told exactly what to do even though they knew, really, what they had to do.

Isn't that interesting? Perhaps that's why so many of us need to be in Weight Watchers or Slimming World and have someone 'looking over us'. It's why we turn to personal trainers or exercise with friends...because it's difficult to do it without strict rules, help and advice.

Anti-dieting values

Many people emphasised that dieting required both ultimate selfishness and self-torture. If you enjoy going out it's difficult. Social eating situations become very difficult and entertaining friends is a minefield. You have to avoid parties and end up spending a lot of time alone. If you don't have someone leaning over you and telling you what to do, this is particularly hard to manage, and it's very easy to give up.

Unrealistically high hopes connected to weight loss

I mentioned in the introduction that 'lose a stone'

comes top of all the lists when people are asked what they would most like to happen to them. In other words, many people see it as the be-all and end-all. If only they could lose weight, their lives would be transformed. But then they lose weight and their lives aren't transformed at all. They saw obesity as the root of all their problems and the stigma of being overweight was what was holding them back. They believed that if they lost weight, all kinds of problems would be solved – from poor relationships to general dissatisfaction with life. When that didn't happen, they felt disillusioned and couldn't be bothered to keep up the dieting.

The ***ways*** in which they put that weight back on (as distinct from the ***reasons***) were:

- comfort eating
- social eating and drinking
- mechanical eating
- alienated nibbling and bingeing.

The reason they make a distinction between ways and reasons is because they found out that the reasons for failure to control body weight were not about the behaviour itself. They didn't say: "I regained that weight because I started nibbling again..." though they recognised this was ***how*** they regained the weight. They were more likely to say: "My friends were all having pizza, so I had some," or "My family disliked the low-fat food so I abandoned it."

So, the reasons were quite subjective... Very much linked to life and living conditions rather than just because they were hungry or needed food to feel better about themselves. In other words – it's NOT just about eating too much and not exercising enough, it's about what happens to stop people exercising and dieting.

Loneliness

Another thing the researchers found was that problem eating and loneliness formed a vicious circle, as subjects tended to overeat when they felt alone and the stigma attached to obesity made them want to be alone and not go out. But in some stories, obesity had a double function: it was both the root of all problems and a shelter against the outside world.

You see, as we stated at the beginning of the handbook – this is all much more complex than overweight people being simply greedy or having no self-control.

So, what can you do if you have lost weight and are keen to keep it off?

1. Find your tribe! A group of friends or a group who will help you. Long-term treatment and maintenance programmes could be particularly helpful, especially for those who attribute their weight gain to deprivation of supervision.
2. Goals should be realistic and openly discussed. It is important to realise that weight loss itself is not an adequate goal, it is merely a means of

achieving something such as improved quality of life.

In conclusion

The researchers said what we all know – that obesity is complicated, and to say it's all down to physical inactivity or overeating is an oversimplification. Various sociocultural factors are associated with obesity. To lose weight and keep it off demands help, support and commitment.

SECTION ELEVEN

THE WORKBOOK

The purpose of this section is to give you somewhere to record your own thoughts, views and experiences. Obviously, if you have purchased this book in its ebook format, or as an audiobook, you will need a notebook and pen.

There's a considerable body of work that suggests that if you write things down it enables you to see things more clearly and understand things more deeply. Obviously, this is not intended as a deep psychological evaluation and shouldn't be treated as such. It's just a way to get you thinking about the things that happen on a daily basis to make you realise that:

1. Things are not as bad as you think they are OR
2. Actually, the way you are treated at work/by friends/in your relationship is not acceptable and things need to change.

If you want to send in any of your thoughts, experiences or anecdotes – amusing, serious or poignant: anything at all – they will be included in the next handbook that will be sent out to you free of charge as a 'thank you'. There is obviously no pressure to do this! If you do send in any thoughts, they will be printed without your name and without anything to identify you. If you would like your name included, please state this specifically when you contact us. The details for sending in thoughts and information is at the end of the book.

So, here we go… The workbook follows the same section headings as the information in the book, urging you to think about the ways in which the issues dealt with in the book have affected you.

THE SURVEY

How much weight do you think you have to lose? (i.e., what weight reduction would make you feel happy, as opposed to meeting medical targets/BMI)

Why do you want to lose weight?

Describe ways in which you think life would be better if you lost weight:

Look through the list above. Do you think that's true? Could some of those things happen anyway, without losing weight? If you had more confidence, could you find the man of your dreams/new job/socialise more/feel better about yourself?

Have you lost weight before? If so, how much? And how did you lose it?

If you have lost weight and put it back on again, what made you put it back on?

What weight-loss methods have you tried?

Have any been successful? How much weight did you lose?

What exercise do you do on a regular basis?

What stops you from exercising more?

General Observations

What have been the moments when you felt you were overweight? A photo of yourself on holiday, glancing into a shop window and seeing your reflection? Anything that made you feel like you were bigger than average?

How did this make you feel?

Why do you think you felt like this?

Did it make you want to stop that happening again? (Refuse to have pictures taken on holiday, not look in shop windows, avoid squeezing past people?)

Many of the things that make us 'feel' fat, are just to do with our own feelings and worries. Do you accept this?

You know deep down that you are worth so much more than your weight, your waist size or your cup size. Please list a minimum of three nice things about yourself:

Have you been to a slimming club of any kind? If so, how did you feel when you first got there? If you've not been to a slimming club, why have you decided not to try this route?

For how long did you keep going to the slimming club? Did you enjoy it? Did you find it useful?

Did you make lots of friends? Was it a social occasion? Did you feel supported by the others?

Are you still going now? If not, what made you drop out?

How much weight did you lose? And what about the club led you to the success/failure?

When you think about weight loss, do you think a or b?:

1. I can do this! I can get down to my ideal weight; nothing can stop me.
2. It's so dull. I can't stand counting calories. I hate being fat, but I also hate being on a diet. The whole thing is so dull.

Assuming you are veering towards attitude 'b' above, think about why:

If you are right in your earlier assessment, and all sorts of good things will happen if you lose weight, why is it not an exciting prospect?

What would it take for you to realise that you can lose weight if you want to?

Work

Do you feel as if you have ever been discriminated against at work because of your weight? How?

What did you do about it?

If you did nothing, why? And do you now regret doing nothing? If you did something, what was the outcome?

How would it make you feel if you discovered you were being paid less than someone who weighed less?

Do you feel that your job has been in anyway enhanced or damaged by your weight? How?

Summer

Do you love summer or hate summer? Why?

What are the best and worst things about summer?

Have you ever been 'fat-shamed' in the summer, when you wear lighter, looser, more revealing clothing?

How did it make you feel?

What would help you to enjoy summer more as an overweight person? (better summer clothes, more tolerance, better range of bikinis, more air con)

Describe your best summer holiday ever:

Describe your worst summer holiday ever:

Relationships

Are you currently in a relationship?

Is the person you are seeing overweight?

Are you attracted to people who are as overweight as you are?

Do you feel worried about dating because of your weight?

Has anyone ever rejected you because of your weight?

Do you worry about being seen naked for the first time when dating?

If you are married or have been married, did you find it difficult to find a wedding dress that you liked? Where did you get one, in the end (a high street store, a specialist outlet or other)?

Holidays and Christmas

Describe the perfect holiday:

Do you think that going on holiday has its own unique issues if you are overweight?

Do these issues have a negative effect on your enjoyment of a holiday? If so, why?

Please describe the upsides and downsides of going on holiday when overweight:

Exercising

Do you exercise regularly? If so, what do you do?

Do you think it's harder for overweight people to exercise? Why?

Are gym staff helpful enough when dealing with overweight people?

Have you ever been to yoga or Pilates? If so, how did you find it?

Do you prefer going to the 'women-only' sections of gyms, or women-only gyms? If so, why?

Do you play any sports?

Were you overweight as a child?

Did you play sports as a youngster?

Eating

Do you feel judged if you are at the supermarket with a trolley full of food, or eating a big meal in a restaurant?

Have you had any negative comments when in a restaurant?

Are you careful about what you eat in public, for fear of judgement?

Clothes

Do you find it easy to buy nice clothes?

Where do you buy your clothes from?

Should more companies produce larger sizes and include 'curvy' ranges? What size should they go up to?

Have you ever had a 'pretty woman' moment...when the shop assistant makes judgements about you and doesn't appear to want you in her shop?

Have you ever been stuck in an item of clothing in a shop?

Do you find that there is huge variety between the same-sized clothing in different shops (i.e.: you're a size 20 in M&S and a size 18 in Wallis)?

Does it annoy you that the average UK clothing size is 16, but that is right at the top of the range of clothing sizes most shops offer? Why do you think this is?

Are you pleased or nonplussed (or angry!) when you see plus-size (i.e.: normal-size) women on the front of magazines or advertising clothes?

I hope it's helped in some small way to write down some of the issues that have arisen in your life, as identified by the handbook. The next two pages are clear for any other thoughts or observations you may have:

If you want your views or experiences to be included in future handbooks, please email everything to bernicenovelist@gmail.com. No details about who you are will be included in the handbook.

We want to keep researching and discovering more about the lives of as many overweight women as possible. Then, we hope to start campaigning for a fairer world.

The more information we can amass, the more ammunition we have. Thanks very much for supporting the Mary Brown series of books. If you haven't read the novels yet, there are many to choose from. See the end of the book for more details.

CONCLUSION

What does all this mean?

It can be difficult being overweight, and – sometimes – it can be dangerous. We all know that waist size is linked to cancers, heart attacks and strokes. We know that. We've heard that, and many of us are trying to do something about it. But it's not that simple. It's no more logical to laugh at a fat person than laugh at an alcoholic or gambler. It just doesn't help in any way. Being reminded, constantly, of the dangers of something does not automatically make you more inclined to do something about it. That's not how many of us work.

We live in a society where being fat is immediately equated with being ugly. When people go on blind dates, they'll say, "Please don't tell me she's 20 stone." What they mean is: "I hope she's attractive."

We have conditioned ourselves to believe that the thinner someone is, the more attractive they are. This has consequences, too. There's nothing healthy about being skeletal, just like there's nothing healthy about being hugely overweight. It's all part of the same problem. But ultra-skinny girls are often praised for their appearance because being super-skinny is associated with self-control and denying yourself, whereas fat girls have overindulged. In the West, in this time, we have decided that overindulgence is much worse than denial.

This 'rule' that skinny is the best way to be has entered Western culture to such an extent that when people are asked what is their main wish in life, the majority say they want to lose weight. We prize thinness above kindness, wealth, health and family. Are we all bonkers?

Before we end this handbook, here are five interesting facts I'd like to share with you:

1. Nearly two-thirds of the UK population is either overweight or obese

That means that being fat, not thin, is today's norm. Take a look at people on the beach in the 1950s. They have skinny limbs and their ribs are showing; they look famished to us now, but they are of normal weight for the time. People are bigger, taller and heavier now.

2. It's not just eating too much that makes you fat...

Being overweight is more complicated than a case of eating too much. For example, the 'community effect' means you're more likely to be overweight if your friends and neighbours are as well. You unconsciously take cues from all parts of the environment about how you should act. We are a product of our environment. All sorts of things prompt us to eat more: not just hunger or greed.

3. Counting calories is a very difficult way to lose weight

Counting calories ignores the nutritional value of food and it's very difficult to estimate the number of calories in food. The average person underestimates their calorie intake by 47% and overestimates their physical activity by 51%.

4. It's an unfair fight

The government spent £14m a year on its anti-obesity social marketing programme: Change4Life. The food industry spends more than £1bn a year on marketing in the UK.

Food companies pay a premium to have their merchandise on end-displays, which account for 30% of supermarket sales. We are not as in control of our shopping as we like to believe.

5. Your brain, not your stomach, tells you when to stop eating

Hunger is in the mind. Dr Suzanne Higgs at Birmingham University carried out a remarkable experiment to prove it. Her team gave a group of amnesiacs a lunch of sandwiches and cakes. When everybody had finished eating, they cleared away and brought in a fresh lunch 10 minutes later. A control group of people with no memory problems groaned and refused any more food. The amnesiac group tucked in and ate the same again. They didn't remember the first lunch, so just ate again.

When we eat in front of the television or while looking at our computer screen at work, we are not giving lunch or dinner our full attention and therefore our brain is not registering how much we have eaten and we may well feel we haven't had enough.

So, what does this all mean? It doesn't mean that being overweight is great and we should all strive to be as fat as possible, but neither does it mean that abusing people who are overweight is fair, or even helpful. We need to live and let live and realise that nothing – NOTHING – is as straightforward as it seems. Losing weight is difficult, and overeating is a result of much more than greed or lack of self-control.

Be kind to yourself and be kind to others. We are all going through our own unique battles. Eating too much is one of those battles, but it's not a crime. Hold your head up, smile a lot, and enjoy life, whatever size you are.

MORE BOOKS TO ENJOY

If you enjoyed the handbook, why not try one of my other books... there are more non-fiction books and novels in which you'll meet Meet Mary Brown as she goes off on all manner of adventures. There's also a romance series and a 'Wags' series.

You can find out more about all the books here:

https://bernicebloom.com/

Or just click on the links after the description of each book below.

Thank you so much for your support.

BB xxx

THE MARY BROWN BOOKS

CLICK HERE:

https://www.amazon.co.uk/s?i=digital-text&rh=p_27%3ABERNICE+BLOOM&s=relevancerank&text=BERNICE+BLOOM&ref=dp_byline_sr_ebooks_1

SUNSHINE COTTAGE NOVELS

Also, read Bernice's romantic fiction in the Sunshine Cottage series about the Lopez girls, based in gorgeous Cove Bay, near Salcombe in Devon.

CLICK HERE:

My Book

THE WAGS BOOKS

Meet Tracie Martin, the crazy Wag with a mission to change the world...

CLICK HERE:

My Book

Printed in Great Britain
by Amazon

42295051R00116